of
WISCONSIN
TRIVIA

Weird, Wacky and Wild

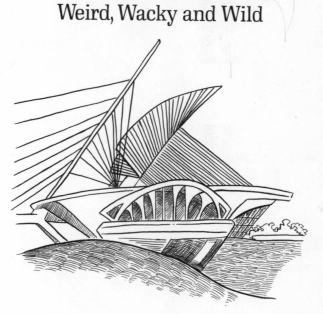

Rachel Conard & Andrew Fleming

Illustrations by Roger Garcia

BLUE
BIKE
BOOKS

The Publisher: Blue Bike Books
Website: www.bluebikebooks.com

Library and Archives Canada Cataloguing in Publication

Conard, Rachel, 1977–
    Bathroom book of Wisconsin trivia / Rachel Conard and Andrew Fleming; illustrations by Roger Garcia.

ISBN 10: 1-897278-34-9
ISBN 13: 978-1-897278-34-5

    1. Wisconsin—Miscellanea. I. Fleming, Andrew, 1972– II. Garcia, Roger, 1976– III. Title.

F581.5.C65 2007   977.5   C2007-905188-X

Project Director: Nicholle Carrière
Project Editor: Nicholle Carrière
Proofreader: Ashley Johnson
Production: Jodene Draven
Cover Image: © 2007 Jupiter Images Corporation
Illustrations: Roger Garcia

We acknowledge the support of the Alberta Foundation for the Arts for our publishing program.

PC: P5

DEDICATION

Dedicated to all of my favorite people in Wisconsin: my wonderful husband John, my loving parents Dave and Ann, my sister Caroline (who lived in Ohio, then Washington, DC, then Illinois...but came back to Wisconsin), and my always supportive friends Michelle (who moved to Illinois...but came back to Wisconsin) and Robyn (who moved to Arizona, but...you guessed it...came back!). And to Greg, Rosanne, Brett, Mark, Becky, Anna and, of course, Charlie. And to Susan for allowing me the flexibility to do what I needed to do. And to Brett Favre... because, well, he's everybody in Wisconsin's favorite person.

–Rachel

ACKNOWLEDGMENTS

Thank you to Faye Boer of Folklore Publishing for this opportunity. It has been an adventure, and I hope to work with you again in the future. And thank you to my editor, Nicholle, for your patience and ability to pick up where I left off.

–Rachel

CONTENTS

INTRODUCTION

"Most American writers are over the hill by thirty."

– John Updike

When the opportunity arose for me to write a trivia book about Wisconsin, I jumped at the chance—despite it being just about the worst possible timing imaginable. I was in the midst of a major home remodel, and two weeks before the manuscript deadline, my hours at my "day job" increased when my assistant took a leave of absence while my boss was on a two-week vacation. Oh, and I stood up as matron of honor in my sister's wedding, complete with the responsibilities of hosting a bridal shower and a bachelorette party and other wedding-related tasks that alone could be a full-time job.

But this was my chance to fulfill a lifelong dream and goal to be published! And ideally, I had hoped to be published by the time I turned 30 (I'll be 31 in January). Although I didn't necessarily dream that my first book's title would start off *Bathroom Book...*, I did feel I was a natural for penning this compilation of tidbits and factoids. I am drawn to the idea of abbreviated knowledge on a vast array of topics as opposed to a lengthy treatment of one subject. Perhaps that is why I have an enormous pile of full-length books that I intend to read (really, I will get around to it!), and even though I worship John Updike, I find that I spend most of my reading time absorbed by magazines. Tidbits and factoids. With subscriptions to *Newsweek, Food and Wine* and my guilty pleasure, *US Weekly,* I can recite bits of trivia about everything from why President Bush has been supporting Pakistan's General Musharraf to how many times Lindsay Lohan has been arrested.

Secondly, I felt compelled to write this book because of my attachment to Wisconsin. I've lived in southeastern Wisconsin for over 95 percent of my life and have spent time up north almost every summer. I knew I had "inside info" to share, but I had no idea how much I would learn. Throughout the course of my research, I believe I've become even more attached to this great state. And as an additional bonus, I think I've gained extra respect from my husband, who is a sports memorabilia dealer, because now I can debate that Don Hutson is the greatest Packer receiver of all time and rattle off that the Milwaukee Bucks set an NBA record for the most assists in 1978 when they counted 53 assists against the Detroit Pistons.

Overall, regardless of the perfect-storm-like timing of this project in my life, I have immensely enjoyed working on this book. And even the *Bathroom Book* series context turns out to be apropos, since I learned that Wisconsin's own Green Bay is the "Toilet Paper Capital of the World." I hope you, the reader, will gain as much enjoyment in learning about Wisconsin's unusual stories, traditions and quirks as I did. Pass the toilet paper.

– Rachel Conard

WHAT SETS WISCONSIN APART

"As I've often said, Wisconsin's greatest strength continues to be the dedicated, hardworking people of our state. They go to work every day, pay their taxes and raise their kids with good Midwestern values."

– Governor Jim Doyle

Two things that make up the very fabric of the state of Wisconsin are the people and the water. Wisconsinites are a resilient bunch—we have to be. Here life goes on in blizzard conditions when other states would shut down. I know people who owe more money (and have put more miles) on their snow-blowers than their cars.

We are a proud group, though never too proud to enjoy a self-deprecating chuckle at ourselves. (Yes, people really do wear blazing hunter orange to Fleet Farm to do Christmas present shopping—that stereotype is both true and funny.) We're proud of our cheese (well, except maybe for Limburger cheese, whose smell is so notoriously pungent I've seen people turn down a $10 bet to eat it). We're proud of our beer, our brats and our Packers. (Booo to the Bears. Wisconsin has a minor rivalry with our Illinois neighbors—hey, they're the ones that drive like maniacs and have weird accents.)

And we love our water. Lake Michigan, Lake Superior and the Mississippi River combined give Wisconsin over 1000 miles of shoreline. Then there are another 15,000 inland lakes in Wisconsin and 33,000 additional miles of rivers and streams. Fishing, tubing, jet skiing and boating are all very popular. And when the lakes freeze, they make great snowmobile trails… and there's always ice fishing.

STATE SYMBOLS

State Animal

Nobody is quite sure just how many badgers there are in the
"Badger State." It's been against state law to trap the fierce,
furry tunnel-dwellers since 1953, and consequently, it is tough
to gauge their actual numbers. Experts at the Department of
Natural Resources guesstimate that there are probably a few
million badgers (*Taxidea taxus*) living underground in the
state—not enough to be considered pests but too many to be
considered threatened or endangered. In any event, Wisconsin
earned its nickname not because of an overabundance of badgers, but rather because early settlers who worked in the lead
mines often either lived in mine shafts or dug their homes out
of the sides of hills—just like badgers do.

DID YOU KNOW?

It is pretty much impossible to dislodge a badger from its den. Their tunnels can go down more than 12 feet and be over 50 feet long. Badgers have even been known to tunnel through asphalt!

Badgers are firmly entrenched in Wisconsin culture. Along with being represented on the state flag and coat of arms, the varsity sports teams from the University of Wisconsin-Madison are known as the Badgers and their mascot is named Buckingham U. "Bucky" Badger. Also, the ferry, the SS *Badger,* sails daily across Lake Michigan from Manitowoc to Ludington, and the "Badger," a Madison-based, mentally ill Vietnam vet who talks to animals, is an unlikely comic-book superhero with a cult following.

State Beverage

Wisconsin has got milk. The hardworking bovines of "America's Dairyland" produce about 22 billion pounds of the white stuff per year, more milk than any other state and approximately 15 percent of the entire country's supply.

DID YOU KNOW?

It is better to reach for a glass of milk than water if you've eaten something spicy. Milk is better for cooling your mouth because it contains a protein called casein that cleanses burning taste buds.

State Bird

A migratory songbird belonging to the thrush family, the American robin (*Turdus migratorius*) has a range that extends from Alaska to Florida. It is not only Wisconsin's state bird but also that of both Connecticut and neighboring Michigan.

Robins are about 10 inches long and are easily recognized by their famous brick red breasts. The breasts of the males are generally brighter than those of females, and, during the breeding season, males also grow eye-catching black feathers on their heads to help attract the chicks. Their annual reappearance is widely hailed as signaling the end of Wisconsin's long winters.

State Birthday

Wisconsin became the 30th state to join the Union on May 29, 1848. The state shares a birthday with the likes of comedian Bob Hope, former President John F. Kennedy, failed presidential assassin John Hinckley Jr., rocker Melissa Etheridge and Nepalese Sherpa extraordinaire Tenzing Norgay, who celebrated his own 39th birthday in 1953 by joining Sir Edmund Hillary to become the first two people to summit Mount Everest.

State Dance

Nearly half of Wisconsin's population is of German descent, and their Teutonic traditions are paid tribute by designating the polka as the official state dance. Both the dance and the music known as the polka originated in Bohemia in the mid-19th century. The name comes from the Czech word *pulka*, meaning "half," and refers to the quick half-step that is characteristic of the dance, which is a bit like a waltz mixed with an Irish jig.

DID YOU KNOW?

The polka became a dance craze that swept the nation after World War II, and manufacturers tried to find way to cash in on the fad by naming a variety of products after it. One of the few to endure is the pattern of evenly spaced circles still known to this day as polka dots.

State Dog

Nobody is quite sure, but hunters near Wisconsin's Fox River and Wolf River valleys likely first bred the American water spaniel some time in the mid-19th century. A mix of the English water spaniel, field spaniel and curly-coated retriever, the new breed was only officially declared a purebred in 1920. Intelligent and friendly, these smallish, shaggy dogs are adept at flushing out both furry and feathered game and also excel at retrieving whatever the hunters hit. The specialized spaniels also fit nicely into canoes and are as happy hunting on dry land as they are in Wisconsin's many marshes.

DID YOU KNOW?

Another distinguishing characteristic of the American water spaniel is an unusual fondness for bananas.

State Domesticated Animal

Without Wisconsin's state domesti-cated animal, there would be no state beverage. According to a 2007 report from the Wisconsin Agricultural Statistics Service, there are an estimated 1,246,000 dairy cows (*Bos taurus*) in the state, roughly one cow for every five residents. Wisconsin cows squirt out around two billion pounds of milk per month.

DID YOU KNOW?

The sight of a herd of cows lying down is a fairly good indicator that rain is on the way.

State Fish

The muskellunge (*Esox masquinongy*) has inspired many a monster fish tale over the years. The largest member of the pike family, the muskellunge, or musky, is famous for its massive maw and for swallowing prey up to nearly its size. These fierce freshwater predators devour their victims headfirst and have been known to feast on prey as large as muskrats and ducks.

DID YOU KNOW?

The name muskellunge is a mix of the Ojibwa word *maashki-noozhe*, meaning "ugly pike," and the French *masque allongé*, which means "long mask." Both are a reference to the fish's bill-shaped, sharp-toothed mouth.

WONDERFUL WISCONSIN

You can marvel at the largest musky ever landed at Dun Rovin' Lodge Restaurant in the town of Hayward. The 70-pound, four-ouncer was dragged out of local lake by Wisconsinite Bob Malo on June 6, 1954.

State Flag

Wisconsin's flag isn't one that schoolkids have an easy time drawing. An early version was designed in 1863 for Civil War regiments to fly on the battlefield, and the current flag was adopted in 1913. It features the state coat of arms centered on a dark blue background. A sailor and a miner, both popular professions back in the day, flank the shield of Wisconsin's coat of arms. These two trades are also represented on the shield with both an anchor and a crossed pick and shovel. The shield features images of a plow (representing farming) and a muscular arm wielding a hammer (similar to the Arm and Hammer baking soda logo and meant to represent the manufacturing industry). Above the shield are a badger and a banner emblazoned with the state motto "Forward," and below it there's an overflowing cornucopia (symbolizing prosperity and abundance) and a pyramid made of lead slabs.

DID YOU  KNOW?

The big white "Wisconsin" and the date of statehood, "1848," were only added to the flag in 1979, after complaints that it looked too much like the flag of New York State.

State Flower

A common sight along Wisconsin roadsides and one of the first wildflowers to bloom in the spring, the wide-ranging wood violet (*Viola papilionacea*) also happens to be the state flower of Illinois, New Jersey and Rhode Island. Besides being easy on the eyes, this purple violet also happens to be edible and goes well in salads. It was chosen in 1909 by a statewide referendum of schoolchildren after more than doubling the number of votes for the wild rose, the closest contender for the honor.

State Fruit

The changing leaves of trees aren't the only source of fall color in Wisconsin. Each year 110,000 acres of cranberry bogs glow red before the harvest that accounts for nearly half the nation's annual crop. It's the largest crop of any state, with an average of around 3.56 million berries a year. It takes over 4000 cranberries to make one gallon of cranberry juice.

State Fossil

The trilobite (*Calymene celebra*) is probably the second most famous fossil group after dinosaurs. Trilobites (pronounced "TRY-loh-bites") flourished in the warm, shallow seas that covered Wisconsin millions of years ago. These easily recognized, armored arthropods, invertebrates with multiple legs that averaged between one to two inches in length (though the largest complete specimen is 14 inches long), are preserved in rock formations throughout the state.

State Grain

When driving through Wisconsin, it can seem as if the state is one giant cornfield, so it should come as no surprise that corn (*Zea mays*) was chosen as the official state grain. Wisconsin leads the country in production of corn silage (livestock feed), around 14 million tons a year, while America itself produces nearly half of the planet's corn crop. Corn is the third most important food crop in the world after wheat and rice.

State Insect

In 1977, the third grade class of Marinette's Holy Family School was learning about the legislative process and successfully bugged lawmakers into choosing the honeybee (*Apis mellifera*) as Wisconsin's official bug. European settlers first introduced bees to Wisconsin, and the state now ranks eighth in the nation for honey production.

DID YOU KNOW?

A honeybee collects pollen from 50 to 100 flowers on an average day at work. It takes about two million flowers to make one pound of honey.

State Mineral

There's galena in them thar hills. Or at least there used to be. Early settlers in southeastern Wisconsin were mostly miners, primarily from the Cornwall region of England, who came to dig out the galena, better known as lead sulphite. By the mid-19th century, most of the more easily accessible deposits had been worked out, and the "Lead Rush" miners lit out instead for California's Gold Rush.

State Motto

No high-falutin' Latin words or pious proclamations for Wisconsin, which selected the straightforward "Forward" as its state slogan in 1851. Unfortunately, this progressive motto has done little to offset its reputation as a somewhat backward state. Meanwhile, Wisconsin's unofficial mottos are generally considered to be "We Cut the Cheese" and "Eat Cheese or Die!"

Though guilty of sending the infamous Senator Joe McCarthy to Washington, Wisconsin has produced such forward-thinking Americans as conservationist John Muir, magician Harry Houdini, architect Frank Lloyd Wright, artist Georgia O'Keefe, director Orson Welles, actor and activist Woody Harrelson and Israel's first female prime minister, Golda Meir.

State Peace Symbol

For a couple of months each year, it is legal to kill Wisconsin's official symbol of peace. Every fall, hunters are allowed to shoot up to 15 mourning doves (*Zenaida macroura*) per day, with a maximum of 30 in total. One of the most common birds in North America, with an estimated population of 130 million, mourning doves are said to be quite tasty in a stew or wrapped in bacon and grilled.

State Quarter

Wisconsin, the 30th state to join the Union, became the 30th state to receive its very own 25-cent coin. It is also the first and only state to have a quarter worth over $1000. The U.S. Mint made over 450 million Wisconsin commemorative quarters in 2004. However, a few are inexplicably flawed. Along with a cow and a hunk of cheese, the "tails" side of the coin features a cornstalk, some of which seem to have an extra leaf. This has caused coin collectors to flip out and drive up the quarter's value. If you ever come across one of these quarters, check for a second leaf on the left side of the corn.

State Rock

The discovery of red granite in central Wisconsin kick-started a late-19th-century mining boom that attracted stonecutters from across Europe. The speckled igneous rock, a mixture of mostly feldspar and quartz, made excellent paving bricks and helped put Wisconsin on the map before concrete and asphalt became the more popular choice for building streets.

State Sister States

Wisconsin has long-distance relationships with states and provinces from a variety of different countries. The state shares symbolic sibling ties with Germany's Hesse state (the birthplace of frankfurters and host to an American military base), Japan's Chiba prefecture (famous for its peanuts and home of the first overseas Disney resort), Mexico's Jalisco state (birthplace of mariachi music and tequila), Heilongjiang province in the People's Republic of China (home to the country's largest remaining virgin forest and an enormous annual ice sculpture festival) and even an entire country, Nicaragua (home to several million Nicaraguans).

State Soil

Antigo silt loam (Typic Glossoboralf) was chosen from over 500 major soil types found in Wisconsin to be the official soil. Formed over 10,000 years ago at the end of the last Ice Age, when glacial meltwater deposited the sand and gravel that forms this silty, surface-level soil, it is one of the most productive agricultural soils in north-central Wisconsin and is used primarily for growing potatoes and snap beans, as well as for pastureland and timber production.

State Song

"On, Wisconsin! On, Wisconsin!
Plunge right through that line!
Run the ball clear down the field,
A touchdown sure this time.
On, Wisconsin! On, Wisconsin!
Fight on for her fame
Fight! Fellows! Fight, fight, fight!
We'll win this game.

On, Wisconsin! On, Wisconsin!
Stand up, Badgers, sing!
'Forward' is our driving spirit,
Loyal voices ring.
On, Wisconsin! On, Wisconsin!
Raise her glowing flame
Stand, Fellows, let us now
Salute her name!"

– Football version

"On, Wisconsin! On, Wisconsin!
Grand old Badger state!
We, thy loyal sons and daughters,
Hail thee good and great.
On, Wisconsin! On, Wisconsin!
Champion of the right.
'Forward,' our motto—God
Will give thee might!"

– State version

Wisconsin's state song has the dual distinction of also being one of the most popular football songs of all time. If a game on any given Sunday has an accompanying marching band, chances are good they'll eventually trot out a version of "On, Wisconsin!" William Purdy, who'd never actually set foot in Wisconsin and had initially entitled his composition "Minnesota, Minnesota" in the hope it would become the next-door neighbor's football song, composed the song's melody in 1909. A University of Wisconsin graduate by the name of Carl Beck convinced Purdy to allow his alma mater to have the tune instead and also wrote the rousing lyrics. While the music remained the same, Judge Charles D. Rosa and J.S. Hubbard wrote the alternate, state-sanctioned lyrics three years later.

"On, Wisconsin" was the war cry used by General Arthur MacArthur Jr. (son of Wisconsin's fourth governor, Arthur MacArthur Sr. and father of famed World War II general, Douglas MacArthur) to rally his troops at the Battle of Chattanooga at Missionary Ridge, a turning point in the Civil War in which Union forces took control of Tennessee.

State Tree
Native American tribes were tapping sugar maple trees to make syrup long before Europeans arrived on the scene. The largest of all maple trees, capable of reaching heights of nearly 130 feet, the sugar maple (*Acer saccharum*) is also the state tree of New York, Vermont and West Virginia (only the white oak represents as many American states), and its distinctive leaf is featured on the Canadian flag.

DID YOU  KNOW?

An average maple tree will produce about 20 gallons of sap in the spring, which is then boiled down to produce about two quarts of syrup.

State Waltz

"Music from heaven throughout the years;
the beautiful Wisconsin Waltz.
Favorite song of the pioneers;
the beautiful Wisconsin Waltz.
Song of my heart on that last final day,
when it is time to lay me away.
One thing I ask is to let them play the beautiful
Wisconsin Waltz.
My sweetheart, my complete heart, it's for you when
we dance together; the beautiful Wisconsin Waltz.
I remember that September, before love turned into an
ember, we danced to the Wisconsin Waltz.
Summer ended, we intended that our lives then would
both be blended, but somehow our planning got lost.
Memory now sings a dream song, a faded love theme
song; the beautiful Wisconsin Waltz."

– "The Wisconsin Waltz"

Not content with merely having a state dance and a state song, lawmakers decided in 2001 that Wisconsinites also needed an official state waltz, so Waupaca native Eddie Hansen wrote "The Wisconsin Waltz."

State Wildlife Animal

An estimated 800,000 white-tailed deer (*Odocoileus virginianus*) roam Wisconsin and are found in every county in the state. Also known as Virginia deer, white-tailed deer are named for the characteristic white underside of their tails, which show like a white flag of surrender when they flee. Males (bucks) usually weigh 130 to 220 pounds, and females (does) 90 to 130 pounds. The coat is reddish brown during spring and summer, and is gray-brown the rest of the year. Males five years or older have antlers that they use as weapons during mating season and then shed. The white-tailed deer is also the state animal of Arkansas, Illinois, Mississippi, New Hampshire, Ohio, Pennsylvania, Michigan and South Carolina, as well as the provincial animal of Saskatchewan, Canada.

The start of deer season isn't an actual state holiday, but it might as well be. In 2007, approximately 800,000 hunters, about one for each deer, hit the woods for the nine-day hunting season that traditionally begins on the Saturday before Thanksgiving.

SEASONAL SENSATIONS

Silly Seasons

Some say that Wisconsin has only two seasons: snow-shoveling season and blackfly-swatting season. Others claim it has four, just like everywhere else, only here they are known as almost winter, winter, still winter and blackfly season.

Going to Extremes

The hottest day in Wisconsin history was July 13, 1936, when the temperature in the Wisconsin Dells was recorded at a sweltering 114°F.

The coldest day was actually two days, February 2 and 4, 1996, when the town of Couderay endured temperatures of –55°F.

The average summer temperature in Wisconsin is 67°F and the average winter temperature is 16°F.

One to Remember

It was the storm to end all storms. On November 11, 1940, Wisconsin experienced its biggest weather-related disaster, which became known as the "Armistice Day Storm." When a warm, moist, low-pressure system from the Gulf of Mexico ran into a cold Arctic front over Lake Michigan, the result was heavy snowfalls, subzero temperatures and 80-mile-per-hour hurricane winds that combined to create snowdrifts over 20 feet high. Thirteen people died on the mainland, while 66 sailors from three freighters and two smaller boats perished in the waters of Lake Michigan.

Falling From the Sky

- Average annual rainfall: 31 inches

- Greatest daily total: 11.72 inches (Mellen, Ashland County), June 24, 1946

- Greatest monthly total: 18.33 inches (Port Washington, Ozaukee County), June 1996

- Greatest annual total: 62.07 inches (Embarass, Waupaca County), 1884

- Least annual total: 12 inches (Plum Island, Door County), 1937

- Average annual snowfall: 45 inches

- Greatest daily total: 26 inches (Neillsville, Clark County), December 27, 1904

- Greatest monthly total: 103.5 inches (Hurley, Iron County), January 1997

- Greatest annual total: 277 inches (Hurley, Iron County) 1996–1997

Devouring Inferno

Wisconsin's biggest natural disaster was also the worst forest fire in North American history. Ironically, the blaze, which took an estimated 1200 to 2400 lives, is far less famous than another fire that occurred the very same day that only killed about 250 people. While the Great Chicago Fire of October 8, 1871, has become part of our collective consciousness, in part because of a myth about Mrs. O'Leary's careless cow and a lantern, the Great Peshtigo Fire, named for a town of 800 that was completely obliterated by the fire, is remembered today primarily by historians and Wisconsin schoolchildren required to learn about it.

Catch a Fire

As with the Chicago Fire, no one is quite sure how the "Great One" started, though falling meteors—common in the upper Great Lakes region in autumn—are now considered the likely catalysts in both tragedies. The year had been very dry, and Wisconsin's vast wetlands and forests turned to tinder. There were also numerous existing small forest fires, many the result of sparks from passing trains, untended campfires and poorly thought out slash-and-burn land management practices. Many fires were probably smoldering underground in the abundant dried peat bogs, and for weeks before October 8, the air was filled with smoke so thick that ships miles away on Lake Michigan had to use foghorns to navigate.

Rapid Fire

According to survivors, all of northeastern Wisconsin seemed to erupt into flames at once when sudden strong winds blew in and fanned the flames. The fire was so intense that it even jumped over the waters of Green Bay and burned parts of the Door Peninsula. By the time it was over, 1.5 million acres of forest had been consumed. Twelve towns and millions of dollars worth of property were destroyed. An accurate death toll has never been determined, because all the population records were also destroyed in the fire.

DID YOU KNOW?

The Great Peshtigo Fire has the distinction of causing the most deaths by fire in American history. While more people died in the terrorist attacks of September 11, 2001, technically the collapsing buildings rather than the flames killed most of the victims.

WISCONSIN'S GEOGRAPHY

The Land Before Time

Over the past 2.5 million years or so, massive continental glaciers have gripped the globe around a dozen times. Glaciers sculpted about one-third of the Earth's landmass and in few places is this as apparent as in Wisconsin. Aptly enough, the most recent Ice Age, which ended only about 10,000 years ago, is known as the Wisconsin Glaciation. Up to two miles thick, the ice sheets stretched from New York's Long Island to Montana, and from Ohio to Hudson Bay in Canada.

Size Matters

Mid-sized Wisconsin ranks 26th in size out of 50 states and 10th in size of all the Midwestern states. The total area of Wisconsin is 54,375 square mile, which includes nearly 2000 square miles of inland lakes and rivers and 10,000 square miles of territorial waters in Lakes Superior and Michigan. The greatest north-south distance in the state is 302 miles, while the greatest east-west distance is 291 miles.

Border Issues

Wisconsin sits beside two of the five Great Lakes: Lake Superior, the largest freshwater lake in the world by surface area, and Lake Michigan, the only Great Lake without a Canadian coastline. The state also shares borders with Iowa (known as the "Hawkeye State" and "Idiots Out Walking Around"), Minnesota (known as the "North Star State" and "Land of Ten Thousand Mosquito Breeding Grounds"), Michigan (known as the "Wolverine State" and the "Mitten") and Illinois (known as the "Prairie State" and "Land of Corn and Beans").

Central Wisconsin

Ever wonder where the figurative "four corners of the Earth" actually are? The exact center of a hemisphere occurs in only four places on Earth. The southeastern hemisphere's midpoint is at the bottom of the Indian Ocean, the southwestern's is at the bottom of the Pacific, the northeastern's is in Outer Mongolia, while the center of the northwestern hemisphere can be found in a nondescript field down the road from a one-horse town in Marathon County called Poniatowski. This unremarkable meadow is where the 90th meridian of longitude crosses the 45th parallel of latitude and marks the exact halfway point between the North Pole and the equator. It is also precisely one-quarter of the way around the world from the Greenwich Meridian (zero degrees longitude) in England. The geographic hotspot can be found in a tiny, fenced-in plot of land off a dirt road and is marked by a sign that not only inaccurately claims to be a "geological marker" rather than a geographical one, but also misspells the word "longitude" as "longtitude."

Bland Central

The geographic center of Wisconsin itself can be pinpointed at 44°26' North and 89°45.8' West in Wood County, about nine miles southeast of the medium-sized city of Marshfield.

The state's setting along the 45th parallel is further celebrated in other necks of the Northwoods. Anyone interested in recalibrating their GPS systems can also do so at both the Half Way North plaque, located near the turnoff of Highway 141 near the town of Beaver, and the Theoretical Half Way Point plaque along Highway 41, six miles south of Peshtigo. There is also a billboard in the town of Cadott that boasts of being the same distance from the North Pole as it is from the equator, when the inconvenient truth is that the sign is actually about three miles too far south, a fact admitted in much smaller type at the bottom of the sign.

High Point

The highest elevation in Wisconsin is Timms Hill, a 1951-foot-high molehill-of-a-mountain found in northwestern Price County. Located less than a mile south of Highway 86, about 25 miles west of the town of Tomahawk, Timms Hill is the only state high point in America that is also a county park. It is the 39th-tallest state high point in the country behind Michigan's Mount Avron (1978 feet) and ahead of New Jersey's aptly named High Point (1803 feet). The park was dedicated in 1983 after the county purchased the former 187-acre logging camp from the hill's namesake, Timothy Cahan. The quarter-mile trail to the summit gains only 140 feet in elevation.

DID YOU  KNOW?

Although Timms Hill is the highest point above sea level, 1924-foot Rib Mountain in Marathon County has the greatest difference of height from peak to the surrounding area. This billion-year-old hill, which is considered one of the oldest geological formations on Earth, isn't actually a mountain at all, but rather what geologists call a "monadrock," a glacially eroded ridge of quartzite. Towering 670 feet above the surrounding countryside, the massive monadrock is home to Rib Mountain State Park and the Granite Peak Ski Area.

Wisconsin's Next 10 Tallest

Lookout Mountain (Lincoln County): 1920 feet

Kent Tower Hill (Langlade County): 1903 feet

Mt. Whittlesey (Ashland County): 1872 feet

East Hill (Forest County): 1850 feet

Military Hill (Vilas County): 1848 feet

Baldy Hill (Langlade County): 1831 feet

Meteor Hill (Sawyer County): 1801 feet

Carter Hills (Oconto County): 1781 feet

Blue Hills (Rusk County): 1750 feet

West Blue Mound (Iowa County): 1719 feet

WATERY WISCONSIN

Water, Water Everywhere

Wisconsin has nearly 15,000 inland lakes and 33,000 miles of streams and rivers that, if somehow magically strung together, would circle the globe.

Wisconsin's Wisconsin

The state of Wisconsin is named after its longest river. Wisconsin is the English version of the French version (Ouisconsin) of a Miami Indian name (Meskousing) for the river that runs 430 miles through the center of the state. Historical linguists have come to the disputed conclusion that the word originally meant something like "this stream meanders through something red," which they believe is probably a reference to the red sandstone bluffs of the Wisconsin Dells carved by the river. The Wisconsin River's headwaters are in the Lac Vieux Desert area near the Michigan border. The river drains an area of 12,000 square miles, approximately one-quarter of the entire state, and drops a total of 1050 feet before eventually emptying into the Mississippi River near the town of Prairie du Chien.

DID YOU KNOW?

According to a Winnebago legend, the river and surrounding lakes were created by a giant snake that once lived in the northern forests. He decided one day to travel to the sea, and the movement of his body wore a deep channel through the forests and prairies. Water flowed into this bed and, when the snake moved his tail, great masses of water splashed from the channel through the forests and formed lakes and ponds. Less powerful snakes fled his path, creating the smaller streams and tributaries that now flow into the river.

WONDERFUL
WISCONSIN

The Wisconsin River's name was first recorded in 1673 by French explorer Jacques Marquette, who canoed up the Fox River from Lake Michigan before portaging two miles over to the Wisconsin River at the present-day site of Portage. He then carried on up the remaining 200 miles of the river to the mighty Mississippi.

Largest Lake

With a surface area of around 137,700 acres, Lake Winnebago is not only the largest lake entirely within the state's borders, but also the largest freshwater lake within the Lower 48. Lake Winnebago is approximately 28 miles long, 11 miles wide and has a total of 85 miles of shoreline. The lake has an average depth of 15 feet and is 21 feet at its deepest point. The world-famous sportfishing destination is a remnant of Glacial Lake Oshkosh and was formed around 12,000 years ago when a pileup of ice near present-day Green Bay formed a natural dam, preventing water from flowing into Lake Michigan.

DID YOU KNOW?

Lake Winnebago was an important part of a trade route used by Native Americans to transport goods between the Great Lakes and the Mississippi River.

Next 10 Largest Lakes

Lake Pepin (Pepin County): 27,100 acres

Lake Petenwell (Juneau County): 23,040 acres

Lake Chippewa (Sawyer County): 15,300 acres

Poygan Lake (Winnebago County): 14,102 acres

Castle Rock Lake (Juneau County): 13,955 acres

Turtle-Flambeau Flowage (Iron County): 13,545 acres

Lake Koshkonong (Rock County): 10,460

Lake Mendota (Dane County): 9842 acres

Lake Wisconsin (Sauk County): 9000 acres

Lake Butte des Morts (Winnebago County): 8857 acres

Still Waters Run Deep

The deepest lake in Wisconsin was created when a quarry used for mining was abandoned in 1983 after the collapse of the domestic steel industry. Approximately 355 feet deep, Wazee Lake is located not far from the town of Black River Falls and was formed after the pumps that once removed 800 gallons of water per minute from the Jackson County Iron Mine quarry were shut down. The artificial 146-acre lake is now a popular scuba-diving destination because of its crystal clear water and historic mining artifacts.

The name Wazee is an Ojibwa word meaning "tall pine." For the record, Wazee Lake is actually twice as deep as the tallest known tree in the state, a white pine that towers 167 feet over the Menominee Indian Reservation.

Deep Intact

While Wisconsin's deepest lake is artificially made, its deepest natural lake is 7346-acre Green Lake, located in the county of the same name. Green Lake has an average depth of 100 feet, and its deepest point is 236 feet below the surface.

Most Coast

Door County has over 300 miles of shoreline, more than any other county in the country, as well more lighthouses (10), and more state parks (5) than any other.

Legendary Falls

At 165 feet, Big Manitou Falls is Wisconsin's biggest waterfall and the fourth largest falls east of the Rockies. The waterfall is located in 1376-acre Pattison State Park and was carved by the Black River as it drops through a sandstone and basalt gorge. The Ojibwa named it Gitchee Manitou and believed the voice of the Great Spirit could be heard in the roaring of the falls. Their name for the river itself is Mucudewa Sebee, meaning simply "black" and given because of the dark tint to the water that is caused by rotting roots and leaves.

Chasing Waterfalls

Six of the state's 10 tallest waterfalls can be found on the outskirts of the town of Hurley. In descending order, Wisconsin's nine next-tallest waterfalls are:

Morgan Falls: Located west of the town of Mellen in Chequamegon-Nicolet National Forest, this slender waterfall drops 100 feet from an unnamed tributary into Morgan Creek. It is located at the end of a half-mile hike starting from a forest road.

Superior Falls: Part of an Iron County Heritage Site, these falls drop 90 feet along the Montreal River close to its mouth at

Lake Superior. After dropping out of a hovering helicopter in the spring of 2006, extreme kayaker Tao Berman became the first person to run the falls as part an episode of the Discovery Channel's television series *Stunt Junkies*.

Potato Falls: Located in a town park about 30 miles west of Hurley, picturesque Potato Falls fall 90 feet into the Potato River.

Saxon Falls: These 90-foot-tall falls are located about three miles upstream from the similar-sized Superior Falls.

Copper Falls: The undisputed centerpiece of Copper Falls State Park, these falls drop 40 feet along the Bad River. The park is located about three miles northeast of the town of Mellen in Ashland County.

Peterson Falls: These remote falls drop 35 feet into the Montreal River a few miles upstream from Saxon and Superior Falls.

Brownstone Falls: Also located in Copper Falls State Park, these falls are 30 feet tall and located on the Tyler Forks River.

Little Manitou Falls: At just 30 feet in height, Little Manitou Falls are considerably smaller than Big Manitou Falls, located just downstream.

Foster Falls: The 25-foot-high Foster Falls are in a remote location off a forest road upstream from Potato Falls on the Potato River.

NATIONAL TREASURES

National Park-less

Although Wisconsin lacks it own national park, it nonetheless has a string of stunning spots under federal protection.

Apostle Islands National Lakeshore

Located off northern Wisconsin's Bayfield Peninsula, this wind-swept archipelago includes 22 islands and a 12-mile strip along the shores of Lake Superior. These so-called "Jewels of Lake Superior" are famous for their sandstone cliffs, sea caves and old-growth forests and for having one of the most impressive collections of lighthouses in the country. The pristine Apostles are only accessible by boat and feature over 50 miles of main-tained hiking trails.

DID YOU  KNOW?

Brownstone, a type of sandstone, was shipped from quarries in the Apostle Islands in the late 19th century to nearby cities such as Chicago, Milwaukee, Detroit, Cleveland, Minneapolis and St. Paul to be used in building some of these cities' most dis-tinctive landmarks.

Chequamegon-Nicolet National Forest

An amalgamation of four separate wilderness areas, Chequamegon National Forest and Nicolet National Forest were both estab-lished in 1933 and have been managed as a single entity since 1993. Both are popular places to hunt and ride snowmobiles. Chequamegon, better known as "Chwam," is made up of three chunks of land in the northwestern corner of the state, with a total area of 850,000 acres, while the Nicolet covers 650,000 acres of northeastern Wisconsin. Their trees are all very young.

These sections of the Great North Woods have all been heavily logged, but during the Great Depression, members of the Civilian Conservation Corps, better known as "Roosevelt's Tree Army," were put to work replanting. The secondary growth forests include a healthy variety of maple, oak, pine and fir trees.

DID YOU  KNOW?

The U.S. Navy operates a low-frequency radio transmitter, used to communicate with submarines and one of only two such transmitters in the fleet, at Clam Lake in Chequamegon National Forest.

Ice Age National Scenic Trail

The Ice Age Trail stretches nearly 1200 miles from Potawatomi State Park in the east to Polk County's Interstate State Park in the west. In between is a rugged hiking trail that traces the edge of the last continental glaciation. The trail was first trekked in 1979 by James Staudacher of Shorewood and was officially established by Congress the following year.

DID YOU  KNOW?

Of America's eight National Scenic Trails, the Ice Age Trail is one of only two located entirely within a single state. Florida has the other.

North Country National Scenic Trail

Wisconsin has the shortest section of any of the seven states sharing this 4600-mile hiking trail that stretches from New York to North Dakota. Even so, the state nonetheless inspired the name for the country's longest continuous hiking route. A 60-mile section of the trail through the Chequamegon National Forest in the northwestern corner of that state was known as the North Country Trail years before the idea of the seven-state trail arose.

DID YOU  KNOW?

The North Country National Scenic Trail also traverses Pennsylvania, Ohio, Michigan and Minnesota. En route, it crosses over 160 public parks, forests, scenic attractions, wildlife refuges and historic sites.

St. Croix National Scenic Riverway

For more than 10,000 years, the St. Croix River has added its cold northwoods waters to the flow of the mighty Mississippi. The St. Croix, known to the Ojibwa people as Gichi-ziibi, or "big river," and once an important trade route from the Great Lakes to the Midwest, also serves as the border with Minnesota. The riverway includes 252 miles of waterways, including stretches of the connecting Namekagon River, and the St. Croix was one of the eight original rivers designated when the Wild and Scenic Rivers Act was introduced by Congress in 1968.

A PLETHORA OF STATE PARKS

Amnicon Falls State Park (Douglas County)

This 825-acre park is south of Superior along the Amnicon River. The park's features include the intimidatingly named Snake Pit Falls and the whimsical Now and Then Falls. The park is known for its unique geological scenery, which was formed by prehistoric earthquakes! The Thimbleberry Nature Trail and the River Trail are regarded as two of the best in the state.

Big Bay State Park (Ashland County)

Located on Madeline Island, largest of Lake Superior's Apostle Islands, this remote 2350-acre park features picturesque sandstone bluffs and countless caves. The panoramic view at Big Bay Point is a must-see. Only reachable by ferry, the secluded 1.5-mile-long beach is a true hidden gem.

Big Foot Beach State Park (Walworth County)

This 272-acre park on the shores of Lake Geneva, featuring 2200 feet of sandy beach, is a popular summer hangout. The water is very clean, making it swimmer-friendly, and there is a large picnic area and a wonderful lagoon for fishing. The park earned its name not from the legendary Sasquatch, but rather for Chief Big Foot, a problematic Potawatomi warrior who was forcibly relocated from the area in 1836.

Copper Falls State Park (Ashland County)

Located just north of Mellen, this park is considered one of the most scenic in the state and features several waterfalls created by the Bad River as it carves its way through deep lava gorges en route to Lake Superior. Known as a habitat where beautiful birds congregate, you might encounter waterfowl, songbirds, osprey, eagles and even giant pileated woodpeckers.

Devil's Lake State Park (Sauk County)

This nearly 10,000-acre park is famous for the 500-foot-high quartzite bluffs that flank the massive titular lake. Devil's Lake State Park is located just two miles south of Baraboo and about 40 miles northwest of downtown Madison. It is the most heavily visited state park—1.2 to 1.4 million people per year—in Wisconsin.

Peninsula State Park (Door County)

These 3776 acres of peninsula jutting into the waters of Green Bay include the 75-foot-high Eagle Tower, campgrounds, trails, an interpretive nature center, a summer theater, a 125-year-old lighthouse and an 18-hole golf course.

Perrot State Park (Trempealeau County)

This 1400-acre park overlooks the confluence of the Trempealeau and the Mississippi Rivers. It includes rare "goat prairie" ecosystems on its 500-foot river bluffs and protects Mount Trempealeau, a mountainous island that local Native Americans considered sacred and used as a gathering spot. Perrot also protects the site of one of the earliest camping spots used by European explorers on the upper Mississippi and continues to be a favorite Wisconsin camping destination. The winding, 24-mile-long Great River State Trail takes you right to the Trempealeau Wildlife Refuge.

Richard Bong State Recreation Area (Kenosha County)

These 4515 acres of prairie located west of Brighton were originally put aside as an air force base named for famed Word War II aviator Major Richard Bong. The park was known simply as the Bong Recreation Area for many years, until park officials became sick of replacing signs stolen by pot smokers and gave it its longer name.

Rock Island State Park (Door County)

This park is for "off-the-beaten-path" seekers: the only public transportation to Rock Island, located off the tip of the Door Peninsula, is a passenger ferry that leaves from Washington Island. No "wheeled vehicles," including bicycles, are allowed in this 912-acre park. Its main attraction is the Potawatomi Lighthouse, Lake Michigan's oldest lighthouse. Rock Island also features 40 campsites, 5000 feet of beach and 10 miles of hiking trails.

Willow River State Park (St. Croix County)

Located not far from Minnesota's Twin Cities, this 3000-acre park in western Wisconsin is one of the most heavily visited and boasts 13 miles of hiking trails. The gorge carved by the Willow River has become a world famous rock-climbing destination, but many also come for the fishing, canoeing, swimming and camping.

NOTEWORTHY WISCONSIN WILDLIFE

Protective Order of Elk

There are a just over 100 elk (*Cervus elaphus*) currently roaming wild in Wisconsin. Although hunted to extinction in eastern North America, with the last local elk recorded in 1886, Wisconsin's largest native mammal was reintroduced by the Department of Natural Resources in 1995, when 25 were released in the remote Clam Lake region of Chequamegon National Forest. Although elk traditionally inhabited Wisconsin's southern prairie lands, today most of the suitable elk habitat is in the north because of the massive conversion of the prairies to support agriculture. Elk are classified as a protected, not as an endangered or threatened species, and it is illegal to shoot them. A hunter who is unable to distinguish between an elk and a deer is fined $2000.

DID YOU KNOW?

Elk are also commonly known as wapiti, which comes from a Shawnee word meaning "white rump." The elk is the second largest species of deer in the world after the moose, which is, confusingly, known as an elk in Europe.

Home Bruin

Black bears (*Ursus americanus*) have always been big in Wisconsin (though they are no longer the state's largest mammals now that elk are back in town) and have been an important part of the state's history. Native Americans honored the bear as a mystical being and only hunted them with great ceremony, respect and (of course) caution. Bearskins were highly valued as traditional winter clothing, the meat as food, and bear oil as both fuel and medicine. European settlers also prized bear pelts as a source of warm clothes and bedding. There are an estimated 13,000 bears currently roaming in Wisconsin, mostly in the less-populated northern third of the state.

Bear Necessities

Black bears are usually shy, solitary creatures that prefer to avoid humans. Nearly all human-bear conflicts are the result of bears searching for food. Tips for avoiding unwanted close encounters of the ursine kind include keeping garbage cans closely sealed or indoors, and hanging food and cooking utensils high in a tree when camping. If you do encounter a bear from a distance, make noise and wave your arms to let it know you're there so as not to surprise it. If you do surprise a bear at close range, the best thing to do is to back away slowly. Neither running away nor climbing a tree are good options, as bears can run and climb trees a heck of a lot faster. If a bear attacks, experts are undecided whether it is best to fight back or play dead. If you fight back, at least you've got a fighting chance, whereas if you play dead you run the risk of becoming dead.

Missing Lynx

Nobody is quite sure how many, if any, Canada lynx (*Lynx canadensis*) remain in Wisconsin. The northern portion of the state is part of the short-tailed, long-legged wildcat's historical range, but none have been sighted in years. This mightn't be as bad as it sounds, as lynx are stealthy, nocturnal creatures that prefer to avoid humans. Their numbers tend to correlate with the 10-year cycles of the snowshoe hare, their preferred prey. Although it is thought that there haven't been any breeding lynx pairs within Wisconsin for over a century, lynx tracks are sighted periodically, and carcasses have been found as far south as Vernon, Sauk and Green Lake Counties.

Advances with Wolves

There are an estimated 500 wolves in Wisconsin, one of only a dozen American states where the species remains in the wild. Gray wolves (*Canis lupus*), also known as timber wolves, are the largest members of the canine family, which also includes coyotes and foxes, and they once ranged throughout the entire country. They've roamed the Wisconsin wilderness since the time the last glaciers retreated, following herds of musk oxen and caribou into the area. There were an estimated 3000 to 5000 living in the area before Europeans first showed up and began indiscriminately slaughtering them. They had a state bounty on their heads from 1865 to 1957, when the handful still remaining were finally given protected status.

Where the Wolves Are

Thought to be extinct within Wisconsin by 1960, wolf packs eventually returned in the northeastern forests, arriving from Canada via Minnesota. Timber wolves were named a state endangered species in 1975 and were monitored by the Department of Natural Resources, which included attaching radio collars to captured animals and conducting both snow-tracking surveys in winter and howl counts in summer. By 1980, there were an estimated 25 gray wolves living in five different packs, and extensive recovery efforts, which included habitat protection and a campaign to convince Wisconsinites to stop killing them, began in earnest. Timber wolves were finally taken off the Endangered Species List in March 2007.

Marten Shortage

Considered endangered at the state level but not the federal, the American marten (*Martes americana*), also known as the pine marten, is a wee weasel about 6 inches tall. Martens are adept climbers, and their preferred habitat is conifer forests, where there is an abundant supply of their preferred dish, red squirrels. Wisconsin's forests aren't what they used to be, and consequently, neither is its American marten population. Their numbers were further depleted because of the popularity of their pelts as hat liners in the early 20th century. Although marten trapping was banned in 1921, the animals were considered gone for good from the state just a few years later.

Transpose the Weasel

Between 1975 and 1990, over 300 American martens imported from Canada, Minnesota and Colorado were released into the Chequamegon-Nicolet National Forest in the northeastern corner of the state. Nobody is quite sure if the reclusive critters are managing to prosper in their new home or not.

Falcon Stress

Once upon a time, peregrine falcons (*Falco peregrinus*) nested throughout the state on cliffs in Door County and along the upper Mississippi and Wisconsin Rivers. Things began heading south for these wide-ranging raptors when European settlers appeared on the scene. Peregrines' eggs were taken from their nests by collectors, the chicks were stolen to be used by falconers for hunting, and the falcons were shot by the owners of homing pigeons, who feared these birds of prey would feast on their prized pets.

Poisoned Aerie

By the mid-1950s, there were only a few dozen active nests in the state. Soon there were none, nor were there falcon nests left anywhere else in the eastern U.S., the result of the shortsighted practice of spraying the deadly insecticide dichlorodiphenyl-trichloroethane (DDT) all over the place. Wisconsin became one of the first states to ban the poison in 1971, after experts finally figured out that pesticides became more highly concentrated with each link in the food chain (for example, from plants to plant-eating insects to insect-eating birds to bird-eating peregrine falcons). Among other things, researchers found that high DDT levels caused a female peregrine's liver to change the production of estrogen, which resulted in low calcium levels, causing her to lay eggs with thin shells that would crack when she tried to hatch them. On top of this, DDT affected parental behavior so that even if the eggs hatched, the adults often wouldn't care for their chicks, which soon died of neglect. Unfortunately, while DDT is now no longer used in the United States, it is still being manufactured and sold to developing countries in Central America with less stringent environmental laws, where peregrines are known to spend winters.

DID YOU KNOW?

The peregrine falcon is the fastest creature on earth. When in its hunting dive, known as a "stoop," the bird flies at speeds of over 200 miles per hour. The air pressure from this bullet-like dive-bomb would burst an ordinary bird's lungs, but it is thought that a series of baffles in the falcon's nostrils slows the wind velocity, allowing it to breathe while diving.

New Millennium's Falcons

Nowadays, the few peregrines that can still be spotted in the state are simply en route from Canada to warmer wintering grounds to the south. While a few nesting attempts have been made in the years since peregrines were named to the Endangered Species List in 1975, most of the chicks have fallen prey to great horned owls or raccoons. However, since 1988, several different generations have been successfully using an artificially made nest site in Milwaukee, which has produced a total of 12 healthy chicks.

DID YOU KNOW?

The Latin name *peregrinus* translates as "wandering" or "coming from away." Peregrine falcons are found on every continent except Antarctica.

Bird Blues
Other feathered friends facing uncertain futures in Wisconsin are the trumpeter swan, snowy egret, loggerhead shrike, red-necked grebe, Bewick's wren, barn owl and both yellow-throated and worm-eating warblers. All are considered endangered.

Crane Campaign
The whooping crane (*Grus americana*) is both the tallest and one of the rarest birds in North America. At one time, whooping cranes, also known as "whoopers" and named for their distinctive, bugle-like call, had a migratory range throughout the Midwest, but by the 1940s, they had been almost completely wiped out because of habitat loss. The International Crane Foundation, located near Baraboo, east of the Mississippi, introduced a revolutionary method of reestablishing abandoned migration routes. Young cranes are reared in isolation after hatching and are eventually taught to follow an ultralight aircraft 1200 miles from their Wisconsin breeding grounds to the Chassahowitzka National Wildlife Refuge in Florida. The birds then return home on their own the following spring. This reintroduction first began in the autumn of 2001 and has added more cranes to the population each successive year. As of January 2007, there were 82 whooping cranes in the program, including 18 yearlings.

Snake Plight

The Eastern massasauga rattlesnake (*Sistrurus catenatus*), better known as the swamp rattler, has the misfortune of being the state's most endangered reptile. The name "massasauga" comes from a Chippewa word meaning "great river mouth." It pays tribute to the marshy wetlands that this reclusive rattler, which feeds on small rodents and the odd frog, likes to call home. Nobody is quite sure how many massasaugas might be left in Wisconsin. Thousands were slaughtered in the late 19th century, when the city of Milwaukee began to boom and the introduction of hogs, one of the snake's few predators after humans, into the reptiles' habitat caused their numbers to shrink even further. Despite their not being a single recorded human fatality from a massasauga bite in Wisconsin, there was a long-standing bounty on their heads (or, more specifically, their tails) that was only repealed in 1975, when the snake was placed on the

Endangered Species List. Although it was initially feared that their population might explode, the snake's numbers have steadily declined in the decades since, mostly because of the dredging and development of Wisconsin's wetlands. An illegal black market that prizes them as pets puts the species further at risk.

DID YOU  **KNOW?**

Rattlesnakes can control the injection of venom when they bite, and over half of all bites to humans are considered "dry" bites, which means that no venom is released. Alcohol is a factor in 80 percent of all people bitten by rattlesnakes.

Snakes on the Plains

Wisconsin is home to 20 different species of snakes. The only other poisonous snake besides the massasauga is the timber rattlesnake (*Crotalus horridus*), which is considered a "species of special concern" because of its declining numbers. The state's non-venomous serpent species considered threatened or endangered include the Butler's garter snake, northern ribbon snake, western ribbon snake and queen snake.

THE HORRIBLE HODAG

Monster Incorporated

The prosperous northern Wisconsin city of Rhinelander arguably owes its existence to monsters. Back in the late 19th century, Rhinelander was just another tiny lumber town rapidly
running out of lumber. Chances were good the town would end
up being abandoned and left to rot like so many other logging
communities before it unless its citizens could find a way could
be found to attract settlers and other industries.

The Monster Ash

In 1893, a local man named Eugene Shepard reported encoun-
tering a "hodag," a giant, lizard-like creature with horns and
covered in coarse black hair, in a local forest. These legendary
creatures were well known in logging camps and were thought
to be evil spirits resurrected from the ashes of cremated oxen.
Some versions have it that hodags actually sprang exclusively
from Paul Bunyan's mythical giant blue ox, Babe, which was
said to have been burned for seven years to purify its soul from
all the various curses hurled at it by its master and other

lumberjacks over its lifetime. In any case, hodags weren't the sort of creatures you'd want to encounter on a dark forest trail.

The Creature From the Black Pines

Shepard described the mysterious monster to a local newspaper as having "the head of a bull, the grinning face of a giant man, thick, short legs set off by huge claws, the back of a dinosaur and a long tail with a spear at the end." He claimed the furry beast smelled like "a combination of buzzard meat and skunk perfume" and also breathed fire. Despite this fearsome description, Shepard managed to put together a hunting party of stalwart souls prepared to do battle with the beast.

The story goes that the group soon encountered the hideous hodag not far from where Shepard first ran into it. While their hunting dogs were swiftly dispatched, and their "heavy rifles and large-bore squirt guns loaded with poison water" served only to anger the hodag further, the group fortunately had the foresight to bring bundles of dynamite with them, which they lit and hurled at the cornered monster, thereby returning it to the ashes from which it had sprung.

Monster's Thrall

As you can imagine, the story caused a considerable stir throughout the region. People began visiting the remote town of Rhinelander simply to see the monster's charred remains, and some decided to stay. It was soon decided that an attempt should be made to see if any more hodags were lurking in the pines and, if so, to try and capture one alive. As luck had it, Shepard and friends quickly managed to find a hodag hidden in its den, which they managed to knock unconscious using a chloroform-soaked sponge attached to a pole. The capture of the hodag happened to coincide with the Oneida County Fair, and the caged creature (which was kept at the far end of a dimly lit tent for safety's sake) was the main attraction. Shepard went on to tour many more fairs throughout the region before returning to Rhinelander and charging admission to see his prized capture, which he kept in his shed. Curious spectators began coming in droves to the small frontier community.

Nappy-headed Hoax

It was eventually revealed that the whole thing was just a scam meant to attract interest to the area. Shepard's famous hodag was actually just a wooden stump covered with an ox hide, its spikes and claws made of cattle horns. Hidden wires were used to make it move, and the creature's grunts and growls were provided courtesy of Shepard's children. However, even after the truth came out and after the original creature was destroyed in a mysterious fire, it did little to diminish the hodag's popularity, and the mythical beast is now the region's unofficial mascot.

 Rhinelander proudly proclaims itself "Home of the Hodag." Several hodag statues and dozens of hodag banners grace the downtown, while the mythical beast is also the mascot of the local high school and the namesake of a large annual country music festival. Even the University of Wisconsin-Madison men's Ultimate team, the Hodags, who won their first national championship in 2003 and are regularly one of the top teams in the nation, has adopted the beast.

Wisconsin Death Trip

While no actual fatalities can be directly attributed to hodags, another frightening four-legged beast is known to have caused several. Wisconsin's most notorious animal is an elephant that went by the unlikely name Romeo, but he was a killer, not a lover. The town of Delavan was once known as the "Circus Capital of the World," and several circus troupes used it as their winter home. Its possible that the cold weather didn't agree with the predatory pachyderm, which killed a total five people over a period of 15 years. He even once escaped from his barn and terrorized the countryside for several days before being captured.

ALSO KNOWN AS

A Wisconsinite by Any Other Name

Residents of Wisconsin are correctly referred to as Wisconsinites. Oft-heard alternatives include Wisconsinese, Wisconsinians, Wisconsinaroes and Wisconsiners, but Wisconsinites is the only one not to draw the red squiggle of disapproval from Microsoft's spell-check program.

Over the past two decades, residents of the Dairy State have also become collectively known as "Cheeseheads." The nickname was born in 1987, when Illinois sports fans, feeling rather pleased with themselves after the Chicago Bears won their first and (to date) only Super Bowl championship, attempted to ridicule their neighbors with the slur.

Homage à Fromage

The attempt at ridicule backfired, and nowadays the closet of any truly fashion-conscious Wisconsinite includes an enormous hat shaped like a wedge of cheese. The unlikely headgear made its debut at a baseball game the same year between the Milwaukee Brewers and the Chicago White Sox. A proud Wisconsinite named Ralph Bruno attended the game sporting a giant, orange wedge on his head that he'd carved from an old sofa, and an alarming new Midwest fashion trend was born. Bruno went on to form Foamation Incorporated, a company that mass-produces the foam hats and other cheese-related accessories. The hats are worn primarily by fans of the Green Bay Packers.

Population Explosion

1820	1444 Wisconsinites
1850	305,391 Wisconsinites
1900	2,069,042 Wisconsinites
1940	3,137,587 Wisconsinites
1970	4,417,731 Wisconsinites
1980	4,705,767 Wisconsinites
2000	5,363,675 Wisconsinites
2006	5,556,506 Wisconsinites

Twenty Ways To Identify a True Blue Cheesehead

You know someone is a real Cheesehead if he or she:

☛ has at least one family member who works on a dairy farm;

☛ knows several people who have hit a deer more than once;

☛ can identify a Michigan accent;

☛ considers Chicago to be "Down South";

☛ considers traveling coast to coast going from Superior to Milwaukee;

☛ can either pronounce or spell Oconomowoc;

☛ knows how to polka;

☛ thinks Lutheran and Catholic are the only two major religions;

☛ was a member of the Future Farmers of America back in high school;

☛ can work the words "ya hey" into a conversation;

☛ considers summer to be three months of bad snowmobiling;

☛ defines a small town as one that has only one bar;

☛ leaves the car's snow tires on year round;

☛ considers going shining for deer a hot date;

☛ has attended at least one wedding reception in a bowling alley;

☛ gets annoyed if you pronounce the state's name "Wes-con-sin";

☞ calls 7-Up and Sprite "white soda";

☞ knows someone who was a "Dairy Princess" at a county fair;

☞ watched the movie *Fargo* and didn't hear a funny accent;

☞ knows several "Why Wisconsin is better than Illinois/Michigan/Minnesota/Iowa" jokes.

Der Käsekopf—German Cheeseheads

Wisconsin is known as the most "German American" state in the Union. Nearly half of Wisconsinites are of German heritage, which made things a bit awkward for everyone during World Wars I and II. Milwaukee, the "Munich of the West," is home to the largest annual Oktoberfest in the United States.

DID YOU KNOW?

After the Germans, the largest ancestry groups in Wisconsin are Irish (11 percent), Polish (9 percent), Norwegian (8.5 percent) and British (6.5 percent).

A Quick Guide to Cheesehead Slang

Ain-a-hey: Placed following a declarative statement; similar to "isn't it?" Example: "It's freezing out, ain-a-hey?"

Believe you me: Attached to the beginning or end of a statement to make it more credible; similar to "Really!" Example: "Wisconsin winters are very cold, believe you me."

Blaze orange: A vibrant shade popular among deer hunters and Green Bay Packers fans.

Brat: A seasoned sausage; short for "bratwurst" and a legacy of Wisconsin's German heritage. Example: "I could really go for a brat, believe you me."

Bubble: A drinking fountain.

Budge: To merge without permission; to cut in. Example: "Don't you budge in line for the bubble, I was here first!"

Cheese curds: Small pieces of extremely fresh cheese that squeak when you bite into them.

Comeer once: A request for someone's presence. Example: "Comeer once, I got a question."

Couple-two-three: An undetermined number greater than one; a few. Example: "We drank a couple-two-three six-packs."

Cripes: A mild Wisconsin expletive; possibly a contraction of "crap" and "Christ." Example: "Cripes, it's cold out!"

Cripes sake Almighty: A major Wisconsin expletive. Example: "Cripes sake Almighty, it's really cold out!"

Da: A substitute for the word "the." Example: "Da guy over there wants some cheese curds."

Fish fry: What Wisconsinites do on Friday nights.

Fleet Farm: A local retail chain specializing in hunting and fishing gear; otherwise known as the "Man's Mall."

Frozen Tundra: Lambeau Field, the home field of the Green Bay Packers football team. Frozen Tundra was the first stadium built exclusively for an NFL team and is the longest continuously occupied stadium in the league.

Gots: Used as an alternative to "have." Example: "I gots to go milk the cows."

Hey: Placed at the beginning or end of a phrase for extra emphasis. Example: "Hey, how about them Packers?" or "How about them Packers, hey!"

Hows by you: A greeting; the local equivalent of "How are you?"

John Deere: a snowplow.

Leaker: Someone who lacks the stamina to continue partying.

Lutefisk: An improbably popular dish made of dried fish soaked in lye.

M'wakee: Milwaukee.

Oh yah: Can be used either as a form of acknowledgment or an expression of skepticism. Example: "Oh yah, I'm telling you the fish was *this* big!" "Oh yah?" "Oh yah!"

Pertnear: In close proximity; nearby. Example: "Oh yah, there's a Fleet Farm pertnear." '

'Scansin: The state of Wisconsin.

Side by each: In even greater proximity than "pertneer."
Example: "Their houses are pertnear side by each."

Skeeter: A mosquito.

Stop-and-go lights: Traffic signals.

The Mil: Milwaukee.

Unthaw: To thaw.

Upside right: Right-side up.

Yah hey: An affirmation.

WILD AND WACKY WISCONSINITES

Spit Shine

On June 18, 1998, Danny Capps of Madison set a new world distance record for spitting a dead cricket. Capps shot the insect a total of 30 feet and 1.2 inches during an episode of TV's *Guinness World Records: Primetime.*

Ballsy Stunt

Waukesha native David Kremer holds the current world record for stacking bowling balls on top of one another. Kremer's record of 10 vertically stacked balls has stood since 1998.

Coat of Arms

According the *Guinness Book of World Records*, the longest recorded arm hair grows from the upper appendages of Jackson resident Jon Sanford. The longest strand found on his furry forearms measured 4.1 inches, a good 0.2 inches longer than the previous winner.

Feather Dust-up

On September 29, 2004, a record 2773 people gathered in Dodgeville to bonk each other with pillows, setting a new record for the largest pillow fight in history.

A LITTLE BIT OF HISTORY

Ancient History

The first European to discover the land now known as Wisconsin was Jean Nicolet in 1634. He was actually trying to find the Northwest Passage to China and even wore an embroidered Chinese silk robe in an attempt to impress the "Chinese" officials. In actuality, he found himself in Native American territory.

Wisconsin has a long history of Native American occupation. Until the late 19th century, the area was inhabited by the Potawatomi, Chippewa, Winnebago, Menominee and Oneida tribes. Two of these tribes now have Wisconsin casinos named after them, two have Wisconsin cities, and one has lent its name to Wisconsin's biggest lake.

A British Colony

As a term of the Treaty of Paris, Wisconsin was relinquished by the French to Great Britain in 1763. By 1848, Wisconsin had become the 30th state to join the Union.

DID YOU  KNOW?

Madison was not originally Wisconsin's capital. In 1836, before Wisconsin officially became a state, lawmakers congregated in a two-story home still in existence today in Belmont to establish basic laws, lay out a judicial system and plan roads and railroads. When Wisconsin was admitted to the Union in 1848, Madison became the official capital.

WISCONSIN'S TEN BIGGEST CITIES

Milwaukee

Wisconsin's largest city is the 22nd largest in the country. It is also one of the few cities in the world where "beer" is the usual reply if you mention its name in a word association game. The name Milwaukee comes from the Algonquin Native American word *millioke*, which means "beautiful or pleasant lands." Mentionable Milwaukeeans include actor Spencer Tracy, astronaut Jim Lovell, Oprah Winfrey, comedian Gene Wilder, Major League Baseball Commissioner Bud Selig, author Peter Straub, fraternal film directors David and Jerry Zucker and folk-punk trio the Violent Femmes.

Green Bay

Green Bay is famous for being the birthplace of toilet paper. The city's Northern Paper Mill rolled out the first rolls of TP in 1902, though it took them three more decades to finally figure out how to remove the wood splinters. Green Bay is also known for being the smallest city to host a National Football League team. The Green Bay Packers, who have won 12 NFL titles (including the first two Super Bowls), inspired the city's nickname, "Titletown." Enviable Green Bay residents unrelated to the gridiron include actor Tony Shaloub, director Zach Snyder and sportscaster John Anderson.

Madison

Wisconsin's capital city is frequently mentioned as one of the best small cities to live in the country. The college town is home to the University of Wisconsin's main campus and has produced such noteworthy citizens as architect Frank Lloyd Wright, playwright Thornton Wilder, conservationist Aldo Leopold and comedian Chris Farley.

Kenosha

Located just 60 miles from Chicago, Wisconsin's fourth largest city is considered by many to be one of Illinois' major suburbs. Kenosha was referenced in Booth Tarkington's Pulitzer Prize–winning novel *The Magnificent Ambersons*, and its fictional family is based upon that of local-boy-made-good Orson Welles. Other notable Kenoshans include journalist Jim Jensen, figure skater Megan Oster, authors Margaret Landon and Milton K. Ozaki and actors Don Ameche, Scott Glenn and Mark Ruffalo.

Racine

There are other Racines in Minnesota, Missouri, Ohio and West Virginia, but this one is the biggest. Racine's main claim to fame is being the largest settlement of Danes outside Greenland. Notable citizens with roots in Racine include suffragist Olympia Brown, Bad Religion vocalist Greg Graffin, NBA players Jim McIlvaine and Jim Chones, singer Barbara McNair and NFL quarterback Tony Romo.

Appleton

Located 100 miles north of Milwaukee, Appleton is famous for being the place where magician Harry Houdini claimed to have been born. This is rather odd considering that he was actually born in Budapest, Hungary. Actual famous (or infamous) Appletonians include Senator Joseph McCarthy, actor Willem Dafoe, rocker Steve Miller and *Fox News* talking head Greta Van Susteren.

Waukesha

Waukesha used to be nationally famous for its clean drinking water, but those days are long gone. Located near Milwaukee alongside the Fox River, the name of the city actually means "fox," from the Ojibwa word *waagoshag*. Noteworthy Waukeshans include guitar wizard Les Paul, world champion gymnast Paul Hamm and comedian Frank Caliendo.

Oshkosh

Famous for lending its name to a type of denim overalls now made exclusively in overseas sweatshops, Oshkosh itself received its name from Menominee Chief Os-kosh, whose own name meant "claw." Famous Oshkoshians include Naturist Society founder Lee Baxandall, sculptor Helen Farnsworth Mears and WWE midget wrestler Little Bastard.

Eau Claire

The drinking water in Eau Claire, a city whose name is French for "clear water," actually isn't any better than it is in Waukesha. The story goes that thirsty French explorers were journeying down the muddy Chippewa River when they excitedly discovered *eau claire* flowing in from a tributary. The city now sits at the confluence of the Chippewa and Eau Claire Rivers. Notable citizens to have sprung from Eau Claire include billionaire entrepreneur John Menard Jr., syndicated advice columnists Ann Landers and Abigail van Buren, and Steve Gunderson, the first openly gay Republican representative.

Janesville

The county seat of Rock County, Janesville is famous for being the birthplace of Gideon Bibles and Parker Pens, as well as the place where Geraldo Rivera got his nose punched in while attending a Ku Klux Klan rally. Janesvillians of note include racecar drivers Stan Fox and Travis Kvapil, poet Ella Wheeler Wilcox, billionaire businessman Ken Hendricks, and Tom Welling, the guy who plays Superman on the show *Smallville*.

SISTER FACTS

Symbolic Siblings

Over 30 Wisconsin cities and towns have symbolic civic sibling relationships with other communities around the world. Some seem pretty unlikely. Citizens of Madison, for example, aren't legally allowed to visit their Cuban counterpart, and New Berlin has ties with a Nicaraguan town rather than, say, a German one. But Wisconsin is undeniably an active member of the global village.

Appleton: Kanonji-Kagawa (Japan), Kurgan (Russia)

Ashland: Takaisha City (Japan)

Beloit: Masaya (Nicaragua), Pinerolo (Italy)

Burlington: Diriamba (Nicaragua)

Fond du Lac: Waspan (Nicaragua)

Fort Atkinson: Puerto Cabezas (Nicaragua)

Green Bay: Delft (Netherlands)

Horicon: Senonches (France)

Janesville: Leon (Nicaragua)

Kenosha: Cosenza (Italy), Douai (France), Quezon City (Philippines), Wolfenbuttel (Germany)

La Crosse: Dubna (Russia), Epinal (France), Luoyang (China)

Madison: Arcatao (El Salvador), Camaguey (Cuba), Freiberg (Germany), Managua (Nicaragua), Oslo (Norway), Vilnius (Lithuania)

Manitowoc/Two Rivers: Hsien Tien City (China), Kamogawa (Japan)

Menomonie: Konakovo (Russia), Minaminasu (Japan)

Middleton: Laguna De Perlas (Nicaragua)

Milwaukee: Omsk (Russia), Schwerin (Germany)

New Berlin: Jinotega (Nicaragua)

Oconomowoc: Corinto (Nicaragua)

Racine: Alborg (Denmark), Bluefields (Nicaragua), Fortaleza (Brazil), Montelimar (France), Oiso (Japan)

Rice Lake: Miharu-Machi (Japan), Sumperk (Czech Republic)

Sheboygan: Esslingen (Germany), Rivas (Nicaragua)

Stevens Point: Gulcz (Poland), Marragua (Nicaragua), Rostov-Veliky (Russia)

Stoughton: Gjovik (Norway)

Superior: Ami-Machi (Japan)

Viroqua: Taldom (Russia)

Watertown: Uhersky Brod (Czech Republic)

Waukesha: Granada (Nicaragua), Kokschetau (Kazakstan)

Waupaca: Rodding (Denmark)

Wausau: Siping, Jilin (China)

Whitewater: Rama (Nicaragua)

Wisconsin Dells: Iwaizumi-Cho (Japan)

CLAIM TO FAME

A Capital Idea

In a flurry of one-upmanship, it seems that every city, town or village has a claim to fame. *You may be the "Scaly Elbow Capital of the Nation," but we're the "Bunion Capital of the World!"* What committee hands these titles out? While many are self-proclaimed, others are undisputed. Here is a rundown of some of the proud, or embarrassing, bragging rights of Wisconsin communities.

Worldwide Bragging Rights

Bloomer	Jump Rope Capital of the World
Dundee	UFO Capital of the World
Eagle River	Snowmobile Capital of the World
Eau Claire	Horseradish Capital of the World
Elmwood	UFO Capital of the World (though Dundee may beg to differ…)
Gillett	ATV Capital of the World
Gleason	Brook Trout Fishing Capital of the World
Glidden	Black Bear Capital of the World
Green Bay	Toilet Paper Capital of the World
Mercer	Loon Capital of the World
Milwaukee	Beer Capital of the World
Monroe	Swiss Cheese Capital of the World
Mount Horeb	Troll Capital of the World

Norwalk	Black Squirrel Capital of the World
Onalaska	Sunfish Capital of the World
Plymouth	Cheese Capital of the World
Racine	Kringle Capital of the World
Sheboygan	Bratwurst Capital of the World
Somerset	Inner Tubing Capital of the World
Wausau	Ginseng Capital of the World
Wisconsin Dells	Water Park Capital of the World

State Bragging Rights

Alma Center	Strawberry Capital of Wisconsin
Bayfield	Berry Capital of Wisconsin
Belleview	UFO Capital of Wisconsin (yet another UFO contender!)
Berlin	Fur and Leather Capital of Wisconsin
Birchwood	Bluegill Capital of Wisconsin
Bonduel	Spelling Capital of Wisconsin
Boscobeel	Turkey Capital of Wisconsin
Boyceville	Cucumber Capital of Wisconsin
Burlington	Chocolate Capital of Wisconsin
Ellsworth	Cheese Curd Capital of Wisconsin (and probably also of the world)
Juda	Buffalo Roast Capital of Wisconsin
Marinette	Waterfall Capital of Wisconsin

Muscoda	Morel Mushroom Capital of Wisconsin
Oregon	Horse Capital of Wisconsin
Potosi	Catfish Capital of Wisconsin
Siren	Lilac Capital of Wisconsin
Sturgeon Bay	Shipbuilding Capital of the Great Lakes
Warrens	Cranberry Capital of Wisconsin

Other Places of Distinction

Kewaunee	Home of the world's largest grandfather clock—it's 35 feet tall!
Marshfield	The geographic center of Wisconsin, known as "Hub City"
Pardeeville	Host of the U.S. Watermelon Seed-Spitting and Speed-Eating Championship. Now that's a "Par-dee"!
Port Washington	Hosts the world's largest one-day outdoor fish fry
Prairie du Sac	Hosts an annual Labor Day weekend State Cow Chip Throwing Contest
Seymour	Home of the Hamburger Hall of Fame
Sun Prairie	Hosts the Sweet Corn Festival in August, one of the largest of its kind

No "Stuck in the Middle" Here

Middleton has been declared America's "Best Place to Live." Since 1987, *Money* magazine has ranked the nation's communities, evaluating factors such as economic vitality, employment opportunities, safety, health, diversity, culture, green space and other quality of life indicators. With a population of just over 17,000, Middleton was singled out for its strong economy, beautiful park and bike trail systems and quaint, small-town vibe. While many residents commute to nearby Madison, the popular American Girl doll manufacturing company is one of Middleton's largest companies. Middleton, which also topped *Money*'s list in 1998, ousted last year's title-holder, Fort Collins, Colorado.

"Best Place to Live" Honorable Mentions

Three other Wisconsin communities cracked *Money* magazine's top 100: Germantown (ranked 30th), New Berlin (41st) and Franklin (90th).

The Capital Brewery, located in Middleton, is known for its beer festival. What sets this outdoor beer fest apart from the plethora of other Wisconsin beer celebrations is that it is held every February. Diehard beer devotees toast their truly frosty beverages in the middle of a Wisconsin winter and even build "cup holders" from snow!

FREEZING FEBRUARY FESTIVALS

Klondike Days

Middleton isn't the only community that chooses to party during subzero winter days. Eagle River attracts almost 20,000 visitors each year for Klondike Days, known for hosting the Midwest's only winter lumberjack competition. Since 1980, the weekend festival has thrilled chilled crowds with its dog weight-pull event and chainsaw competition.

Apostle Islands Sled Dog Race
Another February custom, this Bayfield sled dog race along Lake Superior is free to spectators. Over 100 racing teams and 700 dogs participate each year.

Flake Out Festival

If February is not your month, try this Wisconsin Dells convention at the end of January that offers winter fireworks and tricycle races. If you try your hand at the snowman-making contest, we recommend thick, warm mittens.

Winterfest

This imaginatively titled festival is held in Lake Geneva and showcases the U.S. National Snow Sculpting Championship. Slightly more riveting than watching paint dry, you can shiver as people form dolphins and other imaginative creations from mounds of snow.

WURST IN SHOW

Brat Days

No, a brat-eating contest does not consist of devouring disobedient children. It showcases the finest competitive eaters in the world stuffing their faces with juicy bratwursts in front of about 2500 live spectators, probably the same types that turn out for the International Wood Tick Races up in Sawyer County, and over a million ESPN viewers. It is the highlight of Sheboygan's annual Brat Days.

Going in Reverse

The 2005 contest created its share of controversy, not the least of which was a real reversal of fortune: one contestant tossed his cookies...er, brat bits...off the stage. Despite the unintended "reversal" (which is the official term for regurgitating your brats and is grounds for disqualification), the competition concluded satisfyingly. The undisputed winner was Sonya Thomas, nicknamed the "Black Widow" after another lethally dangerous eater. This 100-pound wonder took a break from her job managing a Burger King in Virginia (wow, this gal really likes being around food), stopped off in San Diego to win a grilled cheese sandwich eating contest, and arrived in Sheboygan the next day to polish off 35 brats in 10 minutes. It wasn't until months later, as people were still gabbing about that contest, when there was a movement to (gasp) eliminate the crowd-pleasing gorging tradition from the Brat Days festival. Clarence Mertz, a former Sheboygan city attorney, deemed the practice "gross" (no one denied that) and petitioned for its demise.

The Ethics of Overeating

Mertz faced plenty of resistance. Cory Bouck, senior brand manager for contest sponsor Johnsonville, argued, "It gives us credibility...this really helps us break through." Indeed, why make charitable donations to an appropriate recipient such as the American Heart Association or fund a minority scholarship when you can gain "credibility" by advocating binge eating?

Likewise, Rich Shea, president of the International Federation of Competitive Eating and the contest's commentator, emcee and judge, presented a case that compared eating to other legitimate sports. After all, if tennis has Wimbledon and even the luge has the Olympics, then the physically and mentally trying skill of shoving food down your throat in record time without "reversing" should have its own venue.

The Brats Are Back

Brat-gobble supporters steadfastly did not want Brat Days to go the route of Kraut Fest—the June Caledonia County festival that, up until its cancellation in 2003, was the center of the World Championship Sauerkraut Eating Contest. Alas, gluttony prevailed, and the brat-eating contest returned in 2006 for what would be its most exciting showdown yet.

As in any great competition, the top competitors are rivals. In this case, Takeru Kobayashi (nicknamed the "Tsunami" after another force from Asia that consumes everything in its path) and Joey "Jaws" Chestnut are the Mike Tyson and Evander Holyfield of eating. Kobayashi's resumé includes records for devouring the most cow brains (you can't make this stuff up!) and rice balls. Chestnut leads in pork ribs and deep-fried asparagus. Chestnut had been narrowly defeated by Kobayashi a month prior at the Nathan's Hot Dog Eating Contest in New York and was hungry for revenge—and evidently lots and lots of brats. In the end, the Tsunami inhaled 58 brats to emerge victorious, much to the delight of his autograph-hounding followers. Million-dollar endorsement deals are no doubt next for this superstar. For now, he has to settle for the crown jewel of championship eating: possession of the Mustard Yellow Belt. No lifetime supply of Pepto-Bismol for the consolation prize.

Deflated, Chestnut explained, "I wasn't able to prepare for this contest like the Fourth of July," leaving many to only imagine what rigorous conditioning goes into preparing for mass eating. "I know I could have done better. That's what hurts the most." That, and his tummy.

Update

Joey Chestnut took the prized Mustard Yellow Belt back from Kobayashi in 2007. The heated battle goes on.

OTHER CELEBRATIONS

The World's Biggest Music Festival
(Also the Best Mullet-sighting Grounds)

Summerfest earns both of these distinctions, one according to statistical authority *Guinness World Records*. The two-week extravaganza featuring a variety of musical acts performing on 13 stages runs every year from late June through early July at Milwaukee's lakefront Henry Maier Festival Park, which is named after the former mayor. The prophetically named Mayor Maier was so inspired by his visit to Germany's Oktoberfest that he decided to throw a similar event in his community in 1968.

Things started off a little shaky, and by year two, the festival was severely in debt—perhaps in part because of competition from Woodstock? But the festival has evolved, with attendance topping over one million people in 2001.

The Summerfest/State Fair/Church Festival Drinking Game

If you find yourself at Summerfest (or the Wisconsin State Fair, or any church festival for that matter), go ahead and atrociously overpay for a plastic cup of Miller Lite and try this drinking game found at OnMilwaukee.com:

☛ Drink once for every mullet sighted.

☛ Drink once for every tank top tucked into jeans.

☛ Down one shot for a mullet, mustache and acid-washed jeans combination.

☛ Drink once for every pregnant woman wearing a bikini top.

☛ Drink once for every shirtless dude with a chain-link tattoo around his biceps.

☛ Drink once for every person under the age of 15 that looks a little tipsy.

☛ At the Fair, buy a round if you step in manure; buy rounds all night if you were wearing sandals.

☛ Drink twice any time you see someone peeing in a bathroom sink.

☛ Drink twice for all those women trying to be J-Lo with the velour tracksuit combo.

☛ Drink twice every time someone shouts "Play 'Freebird.'"

☛ Drink twice if you get spit on from the Skyglider.

☛ Drink three times if you spit on someone—and get away with it.

☛ Chug until the bands stops playing "Freebird" (unless the band is Lynyrd Skynyrd).

Also, when at the Fair, start your own game of "curders," which is similar to "quarters" but uses cheese curds.

Have a Ball!

One delicacy that gastronomical giant Kobayashi has yet to master can be found at the annual Testicle Festival in Elderon. It's just as appetizing as it sounds—or not. For almost a decade, strong-stomached folks have paid $5 each at Mama's Place Bar and Grill for all-you-can-eat deep-fried lamb, bull and goat testicles. Something tells me that not many people take Mama up on eating all they really can.

Eating a McDonald's Filet-o-Fish will never be the same again after hearing one man describe eating a fried ball on a bun with tartar sauce: "After a few beers, you can't really tell the difference." A true Wisconsinite's solution to anything. Five dollars for the all-you-can-eat; $15 worth of beer to make it edible.

DID YOU KNOW?

At the 2006 Wisconsin State Fair, fairgoers consumed 42,000 pork chop sandwiches, 58,000 baked potatoes, 160,000 glasses of milk, 190,000 bottles of water and 360,707 famous state fair cream puffs.

He's Lovin' It

One final note on Wisconsin eaters—last one, promise! John Gorske of Fond du Lac holds the world record for eating the most McDonald's Big Macs—over 20,000! He typically eats two a day. That blows Subway's Jared out of the water!

COMMUNITY QUIRKS AND COINCIDENCES

For the X-Files

The seemingly quiet city of Delavan has seen some strange happenings. It is apropos that the Delavan Chamber of Commerce's motto is: "Delavan—Surprisingly Different." As written about by local journalist Linda Godfrey, there was a series of werewolf-like sightings near Delavan's Bray Road from the late 1980s to the 1990s. All the witnesses described a large, hairy beast with yellow eyes, a snout and a muscular body. If it was a raccoon or even a bear, it deserved first prize at the fair. Those who observed the creature swear it did not look like any known animal. Around that same time, mutilated animals were found in an abandoned home, a cemetery and a pasture. Several years later, local restaurant owners Lenny and Stacie Faytus had a close encounter with a similar creature, though theirs was over 7 feet tall and more closely resembled Bigfoot than Teen Wolf. Similar Bigfoot reports emerged, though never any photographic proof. Maybe Bigfoot, Teen Wolf and the Rhinelander hodag have a hideout together.

Most recently, in 2007, a grisly murder-suicide took place in Delavan in which 23-year-old Ambrosio Analco was suspected of shooting his two-year-old daughter in a van (she and the husband of one of the victims would be the only survivors that night), then entering a home, where he killed his ex-girlfriend, their infant twin sons, and his ex-girlfriend's sister and her friend before killing himself.

Adding to the general creepiness of the area, at one time, Delavan was the site of the International Clown Hall of Fame, a living museum. Images of Stephen King's *It*, anyone? Delavan may have been a logical choice for "Clown Central," since it was the founding site for P.T. Barnum's *Greatest Show on Earth*. However, because of the overwhelming popularity of this attraction, it relocated in 1997 to downtown Milwaukee. A community that attends a clown hall of fame in droves? That is surprisingly different.

The Fox Point Witch

Just north of downtown Milwaukee, bordering Lake Michigan, Fox Point is an affluent community known for its beautiful homes, good schools…and a very famous, reclusive witch. She lived in an old house off Beach Drive. From a distance, the home looked unkempt and rundown. In actuality, the yard was meticulously decorated with unique, alternately interesting and disturbing sculptures that she created herself. Many versions of the witchy legend circulated over the years. Some people said her husband and child had drowned, causing her to go insane and relentlessly produce grotesque and demonic sculptures. Others claimed the statues were trespassing children that she had turned to stone. Beginning around the 1950s and still

occurring today, bored or brave teens would routinely cruise by her home, and every Halloween, a shaking child would be double-dared to ring her doorbell during trick-or-treating.

The "witch" was actually an educated artist and heiress named Mary Nohl. She graduated from the Art Institute of Chicago in 1938 and worked as a middle-school level teacher for many years before opening her own pottery studio. When her mother died in 1968, Mary inherited the Fox Point house and a large sum of money. She spent the rest of her life dedicated to her own art, filling her home with oil paintings and using creative materials such as tree parts, pebbles and glass in her garden sculptures. Despite the ridicule she endured, including multiple incidents of vandalism to her property, she lived a quiet and harmless life. Mary passed on in 2001 and generously donated $9.6 million to the Greater Foundation of Milwaukee to support local artists and fund art programs. Perhaps she should be referred to as the "Good Witch of the Midwest," and one not without a sense of humor. Well aware of her creepy reputation, she arranged rocks to spell out "BOO" near her front door.

A Whole Lotta Cicada

"They're here!" In 2007, Wisconsin experienced an invasion of cicadas. Apparently these little buggers are all the rage. Cicada groupies were breathlessly anticipating their arrival like the mother ship coming to take them home. This particular breed only emerges every 17 years. Not exactly the rarity of Halley's comet, but countdown-worthy nonetheless—at least for those with nothing better to do. The recent faction is known as Brood XIII Magicicada periodic cicadas, which sounds very *Star Trek* and probably appeals to the same population. If you go on the Internet, you'll be amazed at the wealth of cicada fan sites and memorabilia ranging from cicada mouse pads to barbeque aprons—oh yeah, it appears there are plenty of cicada culinary recipes as well. To the layperson, the insects are more of a pesky, plant-killing, garden-pillaging, ear-piercing nuisance, on par with locusts. Along Lake Michigan and throughout much of southern Wisconsin, sometimes one could find 1.5 million cicadas per acre! They are known for emitting a shrill, 90-decibel "song" and have creepy blue heads, red eyes and sharp, translucent wings. File this under Wisconsin sub-subcultures.

The Boscobel Hotel: The Origin of Two Very Different Conceptions

The historic hotel in Boscobel is primarily known as the place of origin of the Gideon Bible. In 1899, John H. Nicholson and Samuel E. Hill, two unacquainted traveling salesman, were asked to share Room 19 because the hotel was fully booked. That chance introduction led to conversation and a realization of their shared religious beliefs. The Christian Commercial Travelers' Association of America grew out of that chance meeting, and because of that organization's efforts, a Bible can be found in every hotel room in the country.

That very same Room 19 may also have been the site of a conception of quite another kind. In 1969, John F. Kennedy was trailblazing across the nation in pursuit of the Democratic Party presidential nomination. One afternoon, the senator and his wife took a "rest" at the Boscobel Hotel where, legend has it, John Jr. may have been conceived.

DID YOU  KNOW?

Approximately one-third of Wisconsinites live in rural areas. Comparatively, only about one-fifth of the rest of the U.S. population is considered to reside in the "country." Wisconsin is getting on board with the trend, however, as its rural resident population decreased by over 10 percent in the last 10 years.

LOVE AND MARRIAGE

Maybe We Should Just Live Together

Fewer Wisconsin couples are making it official. In 2006, 33,437 marriages took place. That equals a rate of six marriages per 1000 people, and the rate has declined consistently each year since 1980, when Wisconsin's rate was 8.7. For more than 80 years, the number of Wisconsin marriages has been lower than the national average. Currently, the national marriage rate is still 7.4 per 1000 people.

DID YOU KNOW?

In 1960, the median age for a bride's first marriage was 20.4 years old, and the median age for grooms was 22.9 years old. In 2006, the median age for a first marriage rose to 25.1 for brides and 26.6 for grooms.

Marriage Quiz
What is the most popular month for Wisconsin weddings?
a) March
b) June
c) September
d) December

Answer: c) September is the most common month for Wisconsin couples to tie the knot.

Divorce on the Rise

In 2006, 16,730 divorces occurred in Wisconsin, or about half as many divorces as marriages. However, while Wisconsin's divorce rate is going up (3.0 divorces per 1000 people in 2006 vs. 2.9 in 2005), it is still lower than the national divorce rate of 3.6. In fact, for 80 years, Wisconsin's divorce rate has been less than the national average. Fifty-two percent of divorces involved children under the age of 18.

Top 10 Most Popular Wisconsin Baby Names (2005)

Girls	Boys
1. Emma	Ethan
2. Olivia	Jacob
3. Emily	Tyler
4. Ava	Alexander
5. Grace	Logan
6. Abigail	Samuel
7. Hannah	Benjamin
8. Madison	Andrew
9. Ella	Mason
10. Elizabeth	Joshua

WISCONSIN PASTIMES

Seasonal Activities

Wisconsinites have lots of hobbies. The changing seasons dictate when various recreational activities are most popular. The state's many lakes are ideal for summertime boating and tubing. Wisconsin also has about 500 public golf courses, one of the highest golfer to course ratios in the country. Snowmobiling and skiing, both downhill and cross-country, are popular in the winter. In fact, Wisconsin is ranked third in the nation for the number of downhill-skiing sites.

DID YOU  KNOW?

The largest North American cross-country ski race is the 42-kilometer-long (that's just over 26 miles, about the same as a marathon!) American Birkebeiner, whose finish line is in Hayward. Each year, it attracts over 6000 participants.

It's All in the Cards

Nippy days also inspire indoor activities. Card playing is still cool, though previously prevalent games such as Bridge and Sheepshead (or *Schafkopf*) have started to decline with each generation. Spades, euchre and cribbage still reign. Poker, a Wisconsin tradition long before ESPN and the Celebrity Poker Tournaments made it trendy, is still going strong. And not just Texas hold'em. Five-card draw, seven-card stud and many other versions of poker are played all across the state.

DID YOU KNOW?

Eleven-time World Series of Poker champion Phil Hellmuth was born in Madison. At the age of 24, when he won his first title, he was the youngest player to accomplish that feat. He was recently inducted into the Poker Hall of Fame in Las Vegas.

Milwaukee is the "Official National Headquarters for Bowling." So how come there hasn't been a Lewbowksi-Fest held in Milwaukee yet? "Well, Dude, we just don't know..."

What's Really Important

Stereotypically, and accurately so, Wisconsin lifestyle boils down to three things: fishing, hunting and beer.

SOMETHING FISHY GOING ON

Coming of Age

When a Wisconsin boy turns 16, he is elated to earn that highly desirable license that is a rite of passage and means freedom to be a man. That's right—he gets his fishing license. Some girls do, too, but 85 percent of anglers on the Great Lakes are male. Perhaps in an attempt to reduce the cliché of a husband leaving at the crack of dawn to fish while his lonely wife waits at home all day, Wisconsin's fishing industry promotes the marital bliss (or torture, depending on the state of your marriage) of couples fishing together. An annual adult fishing license costs $20. For a husband-and-wife team of walleye chasers, it's a bargain at only $31! If you can't beat him, join him!

Reeling in a Good Deal

The Wisconsin Department of Natural Resources ranks its state as the second most popular fishing destination in the country. Fishing is big business in Wisconsin. The DNR reports that $2.3 billion annually (that's *billion*, not million) can be attributed to fishing activity in the state. Fishing-related retail sales account for $1.2 billion, and the sport brings in $90 million in state tax revenues. It also is responsible for 26,000 jobs.

Most Wanted

According to the American Sportfishing Association, there were 1,389,183 Wisconsin fishing licenses purchased in 2005, the third most in the country. Only California and Texas sold more and, let's face it, those states are quite a bit bigger! In 2006, Wisconsin sold over 400,000 fishing licenses *before* the highly anticipated "opening day" of fishing had even arrived. What are these fishing enthusiasts seeking? Varieties of panfish and trout are always fashionable, but out of 162 different species of fish, here's a who's who of Wisconsin's aquatic elite:

- Largemouth bass: The largest member of the sunfish family, these beauties prefer to stay in shallow, warm, even murky waters. You must be stealthy to snatch one up as they have acute senses of sight, smell and sound. Yet clever anglers have a relatively high success rate, because about 4.5 million largemouths are reeled in each year. They can be found in parts of the Wolf River, Geneva Lake, and the Waupaca Chain of Lakes

- Musky (Muskellunge): The state fish of Wisconsin (where more record musky catches have occurred than any other state), many anglers from near and far prize the great musky above all others. About 200,000 muskies swim in Wisconsin, often in the waters of the Chippewa, Flambeau and Wisconsin River areas, but that does not mean they are easy to catch. They're legendary for being feisty fighters, and on average, only nine Wisconsin muskies longer than 50 inches make it onto lucky and/or skilled fishing lines each year. A mere 29 muskies larger than 48 inches are caught in Wisconsin annually.

☛ Northern pike: The most distinctive feature of these cold-lake dwellers is their prickly, sharp teeth. These voracious vampires of the lake with their carnivorous choppers feast on just about anything from perch to frogs and even other smaller and weaker northern pike. While their canines are as sharp as tacks, their brains are as dense as doorknobs. They are the often the easiest of the "most wanted" Wisconsin fish to hook. And as their name suggests, they are usually found in northern Wisconsin waters.

☛ Smallmouth bass: While its largemouth counterpart has yellowish-brown eyes, the smallmouth's eyes are red. They like their water clear and cooler and gravitate toward deeper waters in the hot summer months, unless ascending toward shaded shallow surfaces in search of a crayfish nibble or a salamander snack. Parts of the Mississippi River and Lake Superior, as well as many Door County bays, are prime for targeting smallmouths.

☛ Walleye: Another highly sought-after fish, the walleye has perfected the game of playing hard to get. Practically noc-turnal, they hover deep in the water or in the shade, per-haps to camouflage their large scales and almost metallic, yellowish-brown coloring. Nightcrawlers, leeches and minnows will help lure these trophy fish to the surface. A walleye's average length runs between 13 and 25 inches, and the average weight is one to 1.5 pounds, though 10-, 15- and even up to 25-pounders have been recorded.

You've probably heard plenty of fish stories in your time. So how about a four-and-a-half-story fish? The National Fresh Water Fishing Hall of Fame and Museum in Hayward is over four stories high, a block and a half long and shaped like a giant musky! Inside, tourists can browse the museum and catch a view of downtown Hayward from the open mouth of the "fish," which serves as an observation deck. It truly must be seen to be believed.

Chumming, sometimes called burlying, is a fishing technique in which a mass of ground or scrap fish parts is spread into the water to bait game fish. Whether spearfishing from the shore or dropping a line from the middle of the ocean (where you'd be likely to attract a shark!), hardcore fishermen have engaged in chumming for over 500 years. Debate the pros and cons all you like, but just don't get caught doing it in Wisconsin, because it is illegal—it's considered waste disposal. (Loophole to the anti-chumming law: use a mesh net or some other means of removing all the waste from the water once you've tricked and snatched up your fish.)

Fish Fry

Sixty-nine million fish are caught each year in Wisconsin and, while "catch and release" is becoming more and more common, 31 million fish are kept. For generations, the Friday night fish fry has been as much a part of Wisconsin culture as cheese and beer. Your typical authentic fish fry consists of battered or deep-fried cod, walleye or perch (often "all you can eat"), served in a basket with French fries and coleslaw. If fries and breaded fish aren't enough carbs for you, there's usually a bottomless bread basket on the frequently checkered- or paper-tableclothed table as well.

How did this celebrated custom come to be? In early Wisconsin days, the state's large population of German Catholics observed Lent by refraining from eating meat on Fridays. Food establishments catered to them by offering meatless Friday fish specials. And you thought "Thank God, it's Friday" was just a reference to the end of the work week!

During Prohibition—a blow to Wisconsin Catholics and non-Catholics alike—the Friday fish fry gained in popularity as a relatively inexpensive excuse to go out! The social and gastronomical tradition spread to supper clubs, restaurants and taverns throughout the state and remains a ubiquitous Friday staple. Likewise, good luck finding a Wisconsin restaurant whose Friday soup of the day is something other than clam chowder.

THE THRILL OF THE HUNT

Hunting Widows

To the rest of the country, the phrase "widows' weekend" probably sounds like a depressing retreat for the bereaved. In Wisconsin, it is an anxiously anticipated occasion for enthusiastic shoppers to rejoice. The November weekend that officially marks the opening of deer-hunting season is also the weekend that retailers unleash some of their biggest sales. While the (predominantly) men hunt, their weekend "widows" shop instead and save a buck, in both senses of the word!

For those who would rather bag a deer than a bargain, there is hunting aplenty. While impossible to pinpoint exactly, the estimated number of deer inhabiting Wisconsin woods and fields varies from 800,000 to 1.7 million. Almost 554,000 Wisconsin deer hunting licenses were sold in 2006, and though it may seem like an awful lot of hunters come home empty-handed, around 450,000 deer are killed each hunting season.

Blaze Orange—Not Just a Fashion Statement

Just ask Vice President Dick Cheney about the importance of safety while hunting. In 2006, there were 15 accidental shootings during rifle deer-hunting season, including two fatalities. While that was touted as the "safest" season on record, active hunters must always be reminded of the importance of wearing the appropriate identifiable gear and being aware of what (or who) you're shooting at.

Gobble Gobble

An average turkey's lifespan is approximately 10 years, though that age may be declining in the Dairy State. And hunting turkeys isn't just for finding something to serve with stuffing and gravy in November anymore. Recently, springtime turkey hunting in Wisconsin hit an all-time high. The sport of hunting gobblers has been around Wisconsin since 1983, when 182 turkeys were shot. In 2007, the register records a whopping 52,379 of those big-bottomed birds, 205,306 turkey-stalking permits were issued, and 26 percent of hunters successfully nabbed their prey. The Department of Natural Resources has been closely monitoring the turkey explosion and is making plans to tweak the trend. For example, Wisconsin presently has 46 turkey-hunting zones, and the DNR is taking a cue from other Midwestern states by recommending that be reduced to about seven zones. To keep things interesting, soon several counties, including Sauk, Juneau, Monroe, La Crosse, Jackson, Vernon, Richland, Crawford and Wood, will pilot a two-year experiment that allows dogs to accompany hunters during the shooting season.

A Gray Area

You can hunt deer in Wisconsin. You can also hunt ring-necked pheasants, bobcats, raccoons and even sharp-tailed grouse if you have one of a limited allotment of permits. But in Wisconsin you may *not* shoot a gray wolf! Since these wolves are covered under the Endangered Species Act, a federal law mandates it illegal to kill them. This ordinance has sparked some controversy. The DNR's goal is to prevent the species' extinction by maintaining 350 wolves in the state. The current gray wolf population in Wisconsin is up to 600, 100 more than a year ago, and the result is a rise in incidents of wolves attacking dogs. In the past 20 years, wolves have been responsible for attacking countless domestic canines, killing 123. They seem to be particularly fond of hounds.

Other animals classified as endangered that Wisconsin hunters are prohibited from pursuing include badgers, woodchucks and flying squirrels.

DID YOU  KNOW?

Most hunted animals in Wisconsin have strict seasonal time-frames, permit requirements, zoning boundaries and other specific trapping and hunting regulations such as size and quantity limitations, but the following critters are fair game with no restrictions: skunks, weasels, snowshoe hares and opossums.

TAMING OF THE BREW

You're in Beer Country

Even though water may be the most consumed beverage in Wisconsin, plenty of beer gets thrown back as well. Some facts about the history of the hoppy, sudsy, thirst-quenching goodness:

☛ Two camels, two elephants, two donkeys and...oh yeah... two barrels of beer! Noah was allotted beer on the Ark. Hallelujah!

☛ Beer played a prominent role in many early civilizations, including those of the Babylonians, Chinese, Egyptians, Hebrews and Incas.

- In medieval times, beer was a precious commodity used in trading, bartering, taxing and making payments.

- Three cheers for the "hair of the dog." Queen Elizabeth I regularly drank strong ale with her breakfast. Why settle for tea with your scone when you can have a Beck's?

- "Let's make a pit stop at this unchartered land. We're out of brewski." According to beer lore, the *Mayflower* chose to stop at Plymouth Rock because the ship's beer supply was dwindling.

- Founding Fathers that drink together, write constitutions together. Both George Washington and Thomas Jefferson owned private breweries. Go ahead, brew it up—it's a free country!

- Many brewing advancements occurred in the 1800s, including commercial refrigeration, automatic bottling, pasteurization and distribution by railroad.

- In 1909, Teddy Roosevelt packed over 500 gallons of beer for an African safari.

- After Prohibition, the number of operating brew houses in America decreased from 2300 to only 160.

Miller Time

What Bill Gates is to Seattle, Frederick Miller is to Milwaukee. He was the father of the Miller Brewing Company, currently the second largest beer producer in the country. It conjures up 21 percent of the domestic beer supply.

A timeline of Miller Time:

- 1855: Frederick Miller purchases the Plank-Road Brewery, and the Miller Brewing Company is born.

- 1903: Miller High Life, the "Champagne of Beers" and Miller's longest-surviving brand, is introduced.

☞ 1938: Elise Miller John becomes the first and to date the only woman to run a major brewing company. She does so for eight years.

☞ 1966: Frederick Miller's granddaughter, Lorraine John Mulberger, sells 53-percent control of Miller to the W.R. Grace & Company conglomerate. She does not approve of alcohol, no doubt making her the rebellious black sheep of *her* family.

☞ 1969: Philip Morris outbids PepsiCo and purchases Miller for $130 million.

☞ 1986: Miller Genuine Draft comes out, the first of its kind to use a unique cold-filtered process that protects the beer's flavor from traditional heat pasteurization.

☞ 1988: Miller buys the long-running Leinenkugal's Brewing Company, a popular small brewery based out of Chippewa Falls.

☞ 2002: South African Breweries gets into the mix and partners with Philip Morris to form SABMiller.

You Want a Pap Smear? Ohhhh, a Pabst Beer!

The Pabst Brewing Company started in Milwaukee, though it has long since jumped ship. For a time, however, it was the premiere beer of the Midwest. Pabst beer earned its famous Blue Ribbon moniker back in the late 1800s, when it was called Best Select after its German immigrant founder, Jacob Best. Best Select won a string of beer competitions, including the 1893 World's Columbian Exposition, "best"-ing rival Budweiser. (Well, the company wasn't founded by Jacob *Worst*.) From 1882 to 1916, Pabst even started selling bottles with blue ribbons tied around the necks.

The next century was not as kind to Pabst Blue Ribbon, though it is still the brand of choice of plenty of blue-collar workers, college students and counterculture groups.

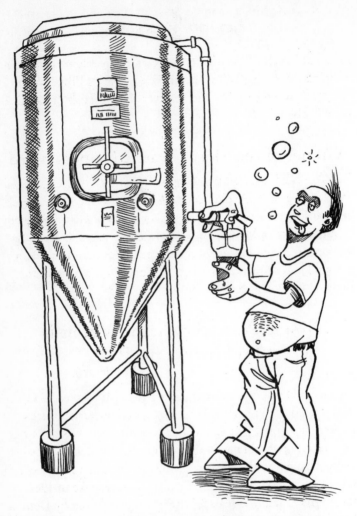

WONDERFUL
WISCONSIN

Wisconsin has more bars per capita than any other state. And if drinking's a sin, the "Beer Capital of the World's" imbibers are well covered—Milwaukee has more churches per capita than any other Wisconsin city!

In David Lynch's 1986 film *Blue Velvet,* the psychotic character of Frank Booth, played by Dennis Hopper, gives PBR further cult status when he yells, "Heineken?!?! F*** that sh**! Pabst! Blue! Ribbon!"

Winner of the Most Creative Names Award

Totally Naked. Fat Squirrel. Raspberry Tart. Uff-da. Unplugged Smoked Rye Bock. And, of course (since this is the Dairy State), Spotted Cow! These are all products of the New Glarus Brewing Company, one of Wisconsin's successes from the microbrewery movement. Deborah Carey became the first American woman to found and run a brewery when she opened the New Glarus Brewing Company with her husband in 1993.

Rest in Peace: Significant Wisconsin Breweries of the Past

SCHLITZ

Joseph Schlitz emigrated from Germany to Milwaukee in 1850. He founded the Joseph Schlitz Brewery and quenched thirsts, for over 100 years. By the mid-1970s, Schlitz beer was the second most popular brand in the country. Unfortunately, cost-saving changes in the brewing process resulted in a decrease in sales. Coupled with a massive Schlitz workers strike in 1981, the brewery's fate was sealed. Schlitz was bought out by Detroit-based Stroh's Brewing Company in 1982. Pabst Brewing continues to produce a few Schlitz brand products, particularly catering to the malt liquor crowd. Schlitz is still often referred to as the beer that made Milwaukee famous for beer, but the doors of the original Schlitz Brewery have long since closed.

BLATZ

Another historical Milwaukee brewery was the Valentin Blatz
Brewing Company, formed in 1851. It became the first in
Milwaukee to individually bottle beer in 1874. Blatz was also
the first Milwaukee beer to market and sell its product nationally. In 1958, the Pabst Brewing Company attempted to take
over Blatz, and Blatz shut down in 1959, its assets transferred to
Pabst. The Miller Brewing Company, contracted by Pabst, still
produces some of the Blatz brand, and you may find it at a local
American Legion tavern or discount liquor store. The Blatz
Brewing Company Office Building and Blatz Brewery Complex
are both listed on the National Register of Historic Places.

MATHIE-RUDER BREWERY

Last but not least, this writer has to give a shout-out to the former Mathie-Ruder Brewery, since this writer is married to John
Conard, a descendent of the Mathie family. Frank S. Mathie Sr.
started small, brewing beer in his Wausau cellars in 1869. He
increased production and his Grand Avenue brewery expanded.
Frank retired in 1892, and sons Frank Jr., Otto and John took
over. By 1900, Mathie Brewing Company beer was so popular
that they were producing 10,000 barrels a year. They built multiple larger plants and established a branch in Merrill. As World
War I put a strain on production and talk of Prohibition
loomed, the Mathie Brewing Company pooled its resources
with its neighbor and rival, the Ruder Brewing Company.
When Prohibition ended, they reorganized and officially created
the Mathie-Ruder Brewing Company in 1934. They produced
their famous Red Ribbon and North Star brands along with
a couple of bocks, pilsners and a special holiday brew, and for
years the brewery thrived. However, as the original Mathie and
Ruder family leaders began downscaling their hands-on involve-
ment in the company and the business faced tough competition
from larger breweries, Mathie-Ruder sales went into a steady
decline in the late 1940s and '50s, and the brewery closed down.

Wisconsin's Statue of Liberty

Each year, 25,000 tourists travel to La Crosse to have their pic-
tures take in front of the world's largest six-er. This roadside
attraction "six-pack" is actually six large holding tanks and can
store 688,200 gallons of beer—enough to fill 7,340,796 normal
beer cans. It was built as part of Heileman's Brewery in 1969,
then was taken over by City Brewery in 2003 and painted with
bright new La Crosse lager labels.

Bonkers for Brandy

Order a brandy old-fashioned anywhere in the country, and
you'll probably be served a look of confusion or a basic "Huh?"
At any Wisconsin tavern, the response will be, "Coming right

up," or possibly, "Would you like Korbel or J. Barvet?" If you order a Manhattan, most bartenders outside Wisconsin make it with whiskey instead of brandy. In fact, Wisconsin is Korbel brandy's number one consumer, making up about one-third of all their sales. It's particularly popular up north where a flask of brandy while out hunting in the nippy November northern woods can warm you up from the top of your earflap-hat-covered head to the tips of your toes, though the idea of mixing guns and brandy might give some people chills.

Sobering Facts

Not all too surprisingly considering its boozin' culture, Wisconsin has the highest number of underage drinkers of any state—almost 40 percent of 12- to 20-year-olds drank alcohol during the month prior to being surveyed. Also, 75.7 percent of 18- to 25-year-olds admitted to drinking in the past month, ranking Wisconsin highest in that category as well. Wisconsin is in the top five for binge drinking (23 percent), defined as consuming five or more drinks in one sitting. However, any Packers fan will tell you that it's not that hard to wash down your Chili John with five or more beers in one bottom-numbing sitting during a four-and-a-half-hour December game at Lambeau Field.

MONEY MATTERS

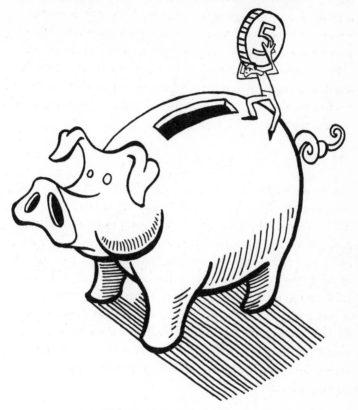

It's All About the Benjamins

Ben Sheets and Ben Steele, that is. Wisconsin's income tax is divided into three brackets, with rates between 4.6 and 6.75 percent. Sales tax is five percent in most areas of the state, with 59 counties imposing an additional 0.5 percent county tax. "Baseball stadium district" counties near Milwaukee pay an additional 0.1 percent tax to support Miller Park (you're welcome, Ben Sheets and friends), and Brown County pays an extra 0.5 percent football stadium tax (you're welcome, Ben Steele—well, until you got traded to the Texans).

Not Working But Not Poor

At 5.1 percent, Wisconsin has one of the top 10 highest unemployment rates in the country. Ouch. On the other hand, only 8.7 percent of Wisconsinites are living at or below the poverty level, compared to 12.4 percent nationwide.

House and Home

The median annual household income of $43,800 in Wisconsin is slightly higher than the $42,000 national median income. Furthermore, Wisconsin ranks 14th highest out of all the states in home ownership.

DID YOU  KNOW?

Wisconsin's total gross state product is over $211 billion, the 19th highest in the U.S. Its three leading industries are agriculture, manufacturing and tourism.

FUNNY FARMS

Dairy Dominates

For 160 years, agriculture has been one of Wisconsin's primary economic sources. The dairy industry employs 160,000 people, accounting for about 4.6 percent of all jobs in the state and employing one in eight people. Wisconsin's $20.6 billion dairy industry crushes Florida's $9 billion orange industry and Idaho's $2.5 billion potato industry.

DID YOU  KNOW?

Over 99 percent of Wisconsin dairy farms are family owned.

Holy Cow!

With 1.3 million dairy cows grazing this great state, there's a reason why Wisconsin has been officially know since 1930 as "America's Dairyland." (It is even proclaimed on Wisconsin license plates!) Wisconsin cows produce 1.8 billion pounds of milk each month! Here are more interesting facts about our spotted friends:

☛ The average dairy cow weighs 1400 pounds and produces 2221 gallons of milk each year. That ends up generating about $17,000 per year in economic impact.

☛ Wisconsin has 23 dairy cows per square mile, more than any other state. Its cows are responsible for about 15 percent of the total milk supply in the United States.

☛ There's not a lot of variety in a cow's life. Cows spend approximately six hours a day eating and an additional eight hours chewing. They are milked at least twice a day.

☞ Wisconsin's major breeds of cattle are Ayrshire, Brown Swiss, Guernsey, Holstein, Jersey and Milking Shorthorn.

☞ Cow tipping is most likely an urban (or actually "rural") legend. According to scientists, the mass of a cow would require several humans to exert enough force to tip it. And they'd have to work very quickly. Since cows do not, in fact, sleep standing up, but merely doze, the cow would most likely react and just walk away.

Just Say "Cheese"!

With over 2.5 billion pounds each year, Wisconsin is the nation's current champ of cheese production, though the race is a lot tighter than you might think. Last year, California produced a whopping 2.1 billion pounds of cheese and may very well soon surpass Wisconsin in output. Even if the numbers don't support the Big Cheese title, Wisconsin's culture always will. And while the Golden State produces around 200 cheese varieties, Wisconsin produces over 600 different forms and styles. Wisconsin has 18,000 dairy farms and 126 cheese plants. That's a lot of cheese.

DID YOU KNOW?

The average American eats approximately 30 pounds of cheese each year and will consume about a ton in a lifetime.

Cheesy Comment

"Washington, DC, is to lying what Wisconsin is to cheese."

– Dennis Miller, comedian, talk show host and political commentator

Wisconsin is the number one United States supplier of Muenster (67 percent), brick (43 percent), Cheddar (26 percent) and mozzarella (25 percent).

DID YOU KNOW?

Colby, in 1874, and brick, in 1875, are the only cheeses that were invented in Wisconsin. The name "brick" comes from the cheesemaking practice of using actual bricks to press moisture from the cheese.

Not Just Any Cheese Cuts the Mustard

In 1921, Wisconsin became the first state to grade cheese for quality, and today, the state still has the strictest cheesemaking and dairy product quality standards in the country. In the 2006 World Championship Cheese Contest, Wisconsin cheesemakers received 57 awards, more than any other state or country.

Cheese curds are popcorn-sized chunks of very fresh, young Cheddar cheese. They are served in their natural state, before the cheese would otherwise be processed into blocks and aged. The true test to discern if a cheese curd is fresh is that it should squeak when you bite into it! Any real Wisconsinite has also had fried cheese curds—curds that are beer-battered and deep-fried. Your waistline won't thank you, but your taste buds sure will!

How Do I Get My Cheesemaker's License?

Wisconsin has 1290 licensed cheesemakers, more than any other state. Obtaining your license to cheese is not quite like taking the bar exam, but Wisconsin take its cheese pretty seriously.

To become a cheesemaker, you have to pass a written exam that covers:

☛ Cheesemaking laws related to sanitation, composition and labeling, among others;

☛ Cheesemaking fundamentals such as the preparation of equipment, controlling acidity, yeast and mold, and common cheese defects and how to overcome them;

☛ And for the math portion, arithmetic problems relevant to dairy production.

Prospective cheesemakers must demonstrate a practical working knowledge of pasteurization, milk grading and cheese analysis, including the nerve-wracking judging of cheese samples.

You must also complete an 18-month internship under a licensed cheesemaker or a combination of an internship and credits in dairy-related coursework from an accredited college or university.

Lastly, the license will cost you $60.

DID YOU  **KNOW?**

Carie Wagner was the first woman ever to earn the title of Master Cheesemaker from the University of Wisconsin-Madison in 2001.

You Scream, I Scream

Ice cream also has a long tradition of popularity in Wisconsin. Wisconsinites consume nearly 21 million gallons of ice cream each year. A Milwaukee staple is Kopp's Frozen Custard, founded in 1950, which operates three locations where patrons can enjoy old-fashioned jumbo burgers and unique custard flavors such as "Cotton Candy Confetti" and "Rum and Coca-Cola."

Culver's

Craig Culver opened the first Culver's at the site of an old A&W Restaurant in Sauk City in 1984. Other parts of the country can have a taste of Wisconsin at one of the 330 Culver's locations in 16 states. They serve milkshakes, butter burgers, fried cheese curds and, of course, custard.

How the Ice Cream Sundae Came to Be

In Two Rivers, freethinking George Hallover was the first customer to request chocolate sauce, typically used for ice cream sodas, on top of his ice cream. For the cost of a nickel, soda fountain owner Edward Berner obliged. Berner began offering this new concoction on Sundays. The salesman who ordered oblong dishes in which to serve the treat called the glassware "sundae dishes."

Malted milk was originally conceived by Racine brothers William and James Horlick as a high-protein, easy-to-digest baby formula. They called it "diastoid," which could have been a disaster, but by 1887, they realized that the powder was a better fit for soda fountains, and it was renamed "malted milk."

THE HERBAL WONDER

They're Feeling Pretty Randy Up in Marathon County

Ginseng, a natural herb used in tea and herbal remedies, is often believed to be an aphrodisiac. American ginseng (*Panax quinquefolius*), also known as Wisconsin ginseng, is grown in large quantities in Wausau and other parts of Marathon County. Back in 1904, the Fromm brothers transplanted 100 wild ginseng plants and were the first farmers to successfully harvest the plant in Wisconsin. Today, Marathon County has 3000 acres of ginseng farmland and produces almost 1.5 million pounds of the herb annually.

Wisconsin ginseng has very high levels of ginsenoside (the active ingredient), and its unique, highly prized bitter flavor has earned it a reputation for being the best in the world.

DID YOU KNOW?

It is a common misconception that ginseng comes primarily from Asia. In fact, Marathon County regularly ships a great deal of ginseng to Hong Kong.

MANLY MANUFACTURING

Plenty of Paper

What do diapers, laminate-floor backing, gum wrappers and microwave popcorn bags have in common? They all might be made from Wisconsin paper! With 15 million acres of forest land, Wisconsin produces 5.3 million tons of paper a year.

But what about the trees? To maintain ecological balance, paper companies plant over eight million seedlings annually.

Wisconsin is the nation's number one manufacturer of mining machinery, low-horsepower gasoline engines, x-ray equipment and power cranes.

Cheesy Riders

Milwaukee is Grand Central Station for leather, tattoos and 'do rags. In other words, motorcycle manufacturer Harley-Davidson. Though in 2003, the people at Harley-Davidson

committed a bit of a faux pas. Over 250,000 Harley fans flocked to Milwaukee over Labor Day weekend to kick off the Open Road Tour with "Harley Fest," a celebration of Harley's 100th anniversary. For weeks, if not months, the Harley PR people hinted at who would be the big "mystery guest" to perform at the closing night. People giddily speculated...George Thorogood? Ted Nugent?? "Born to be Wild's" Steppenwolf???

After much buildup and anticipation, the opening acts received a moderate reception. Tim McGraw...all right. And Kid Rock. Those in attendance probably had teenagers at home that would have appreciated him more, but he wasn't the worst choice in the world. No, the worst choice in the world turned out to be the secret headliner—Sir Elton John. Whatever PR genius thought a pudgy, British love-song-belter and piano player would excite a mob of bikers must have been breathing too many chopper fumes.

The first hydroelectric power plant was constructed in Appleton in 1882. By harnessing the power of running water, the plant created electricity that powered two paper mills and one mill owner's private residence. In total, it produced 12.5 kilowatts. Today's plants generate from several hundred kilowatts up to several hundred megawatts. Hydropower accounts for 49 percent of all reusable energy in America.

Boxers or Briefs?

Jockey International, based in Kenosha, invented the first "briefs" underwear in 1934. They were an instant success, selling out at almost every retailer. Today's briefs are still by far the most popular male support choice, with 57 percent of men preferring briefs over tight boxers (18 percent) or loose boxers (29 percent).

WISCONSIN DELLS

Picture Perfect

The Dells is a marriage of natural beauty and kitschy tourism. One of the early pioneers of Dells tourism, photographer H.H. Bennett, opened a studio in 1875 to share his groundbreaking photographs of the "dells" themselves, jaw-dropping sandstone formations along the Wisconsin River, and other scenic wonders that lured travelers to the area. He is often credited with inventing many parts of the modern camera, and today the H.H. Bennett Museum, located in the Dells, still displays much of his work.

Not far from the Dells, one can find the House on the Rock, a true sight to be seen. Designed by Alex Jordan Jr. and sitting literally atop a 60-foot-high rock column, the branching complex has 14 rooms and contains numerous historical collectibles such as unique musical instruments and nautical and aviation exhibits. The world's largest carousel can also be seen at the House on the Rock.

Water World

For 50 years, tourists explored the spectacular views of the Dells while on Wisconsin Ducks Tours, which cover both land and water. For the kids, Noah's Ark claims to be the world's largest outdoor water park and continues to be a popular choice since it opened in 1979. More recently, the Kalahari Resort was constructed and offers the nation's largest indoor water park.

Something for Everyone

Some view the Dells as a modern resort destination for families on a modest budget—once they get through the traffic that clogs the main downtown drag during peak season. Others enjoy the primal carnival aura of many attractions and the rare finds that lurk in the quaint antique shops. Either way, over five million Dells dwellers visit each year.

FAMOUS NAMES

Gibraltar (Not the Strait or the Rock) and Brussels (Not the One in Belgium)

With its 250 miles of shoreline and 10 lighthouses, Door County is also a popular regional tourist destination. During the prime summer months, the population inhabiting the peninsula sky-rockets from around 30,000 to 250,000 tourists, workers and fair-weather residents. Gibraltar, Brussels, Egg Harbor and Bailey's Harbor are just a few of the areas visitors flock to for fish boils, cherry orchards, wineries and cozy bed and breakfasts. Make sure you check out Al Johnson's Swedish Restaurant in Sister Bay. In 2007, this "Door County icon" officially joined the Visitor's Bureau. Its main attraction? You don't hear much about the food, though one would expect decent pancakes and Swedish meatballs. But the reason for all the hoopla is because live goats graze on the sod-covered restaurant rooftop. Hey, most touristy spots have a gimmick, and Al's is goats on the roof. Apparently people come from miles around to see Cooper and Flipper and company. Just make sure they don't spit on you.

Lake Geneva (Not the One in Switzerland or France)

Lake Geneva, Wisconsin, is another getaway spot that tends to attract mini-vans and SUVs from Chicago, Milwaukee, Madison and the Twin Cities. There are many wonderful shops along Main Street and appealing resorts right on the lake, which is actually called Geneva Lake. One unusual tradition that Lake Geneva has continued since 1870—*Walworth*, the famous mail boat! During the warm months, the *Walworth* ships out at 10:00 AM each day and cruises along the lake. Without even stopping, the mail carrier hops off to make deliveries at each of about 60 homes and jumps back onto the boat to continue the route. No other postal system delivers utility bills and *US Weekly* magazines quite like that. It's also the only mail "truck" that hosts cocktail receptions!

TEN OF WISCONSIN'S BIGGEST THINGS

World's Tallest Talking Cow

Although the world's all-time heftiest heifer is the statue known as "Salem Sue" in North Dakota, Neillsville's "Chatty Belle" is the largest that is fitted with speakers and recorded messages. At the push of a button, the 16-foot-tall cow (seven times as large as the average Holstein) will share her opinions on the merits of eating cheese and offer a variety of dairy-related facts.

World's Largest Artificial Cheese

The Clark County town of Neillsville is home to yet another towering totem celebrating the agricultural area's milky ways. Neillsville's other big draw is the big cheese. The monument commemorates a 34,591-pound Cheddar churned out by local manufacturer Steve's Cheese for the 1964 World's Fair in New York. The chunky cheese was ultimately eaten afterward, so a 14.5-by-6.5-by-5.5-foot polystyrene wedge was constructed and put on proud display atop a trailer bed so that the momentous cheese wouldn't be forgotten. And, as if a replica of the giant red-letter cheddar wasn't enough to entice visitors into town, in front of it sits the world's smallest replica of the replica of the world's largest piece of cheese. They don't call Wisconsin "America's Dairyland" for nothing!

World's Largest Four-Sided Clock

While not as famous as London's Big Ben, the clock faces of the Allen-Bradley Clock Tower in downtown Milwaukee are nearly twice the size of its English cousin. Nicknamed the "Polish Moon" for the predominantly Polish neighborhood that it looms over, the clock's hour hands are over 15 feet long and weigh

490 pounds each. The towering timepiece's lit faces have served as a handy nighttime navigation aid for Lake Michigan sailors since its construction in 1962.

World's Largest Penny
They say every penny counts, but few count quite so much as the one in the northern Wisconsin town of Woodruff. The world's biggest one-cent coin commemorates a 1953 fundraising drive organized by a local physician, Kate Pelham Newcomb, who asked the town's schoolchildren to save their pennies to help pay for the construction of a much-needed hospital. After a local TV station reported the story, it went national, and

pennies began pouring in from all over the country. Nearly two million copper pieces were tallied in total—enough to earn the town its medical center. The concrete commemorative coin is located at the corner of 3rd Avenue and Hemlock Street in front of a retirement home named for the good doctor (it is also most likely now home to some of the original penny-pinching school-children).

World's Largest Scrap Metal Sculpture

It is debatable whether the Forevertron is, as claimed, an actual antigravity machine intended to propel its creator, a Victorian-era British time traveler named Dr. Evermor, into the cosmos on a magnetic lightning force beam. What is not debatable is that the four-story, 320-ton sculpture, located in the fantastical

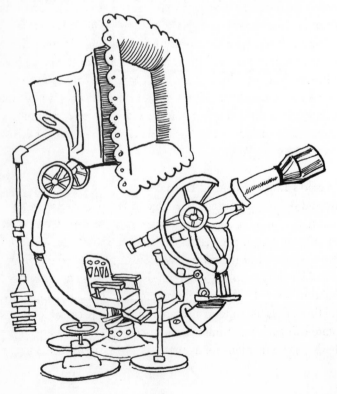

Dickeyville Grotto just south of Baraboo, is the largest of its kind on the planet. Almost all the components of the Forevertron are 50 to 100 years old, including two electricity-producing dynamos built by Thomas Edison and the decontamination chamber from the Apollo space missions. The sculpture includes also ray guns, a giant telescope, a viewing platform intended for Queen Victoria and Prince Albert and a giant glass ball shrouded in a copper egg. Although the largest, the Forevertron is only one of dozens of scrap metal sculptures on display created by artist Tom Every, also known as Dr. Evermor.

World's Most Massive Mustard Collection

The story goes that the colossal condiment collection began after a Red Sox fan named Barry Levenson was found despondently roaming the aisles of an all-night grocery store after his team lost the seventh game of the 1986 World Series. He heard a voice coming from the mustard shelf saying, "If you collect us, they will come," and the rest is local history. Levenson's Mustard Museum, located on Main Street in Mount Horeb, now houses more than 3500 types of mustard from all 50 states and 60 different countries, as well as items of historical mustard importance such as vintage pots and advertisements. And, yes, they have Grey Poupon.

World's Largest Round Barn

Round barns were once all the rage in farming circles, before automated milking machines made them obsolete. Constructed in 1916 for the then-considerable sum of $5000, the Round Barn is located in the central Wisconsin town of Marshfield. The two-story barn is 150 feet in diameter and was built by hand by a band of barn-building brothers without using scaffolding or visible support beams. It hosts the Central Wisconsin State Fair each year and has enough seating for 1000 people. It also has stanchions for as many as 250 head of cattle.

World's Largest Experimental Air Show

For one week every summer, the control tower at Wittman Regional Airport in Oshkosh becomes the busiest of its kind in the world. The annual Experimental Aircraft Association AirVenture, which first debuted in 1953, now attracts over 10,000 airplanes and nearly half a million aviation enthusiasts. The event, centered around mostly homebuilt, vintage and modified aircraft, injects an estimated $80 million into Wisconsin's coffers. Highlights of recent years include appearances of the Rutan *Voyager* (the first aircraft to fly around the world without refueling), the British Concorde jet, a massive Airbus Beluga cargo jet, Lockheed's U-2 spy plane, the F-22 Raptor, NASA's Super Guppy and, in 2003, a replica of the Wright Brothers' famous Flyer to celebrate the centennial of airplanes.

World's Most Massive Letter "M"

On a sunny spring day in 1937, a group of hikers from Platteville stopped for a break on the side of the Platte Mound, a 150-foot-tall hill that looms over this small southwestern mining town. For whatever reason, they decided to gather rocks and build a giant letter "M." By the end of the day, they'd completed the first leg of the letter, which was about 15 feet wide and 60 feet long. Their efforts drew the attention the director of the nearby

University of Wisconsin's local School of Mines, who decided to put the entire student body to work completing the "M," which also happened to be the mining school's monogram. Using picks, crowbars and wheelbarrows, students moved some 400 tons of limestone rocks to create an "M" that is 241 feet high and 214 feet wide. The colossal character receives a fresh coat of paint each year and is visible from just about everywhere in town. It positively dwarfs the town's second largest "M," the golden arches of the McDonald's restaurant on Highway 151.

World's Largest Trivia Contest

Apart from the unofficial nightly *Jeopardy* audience, the largest celebration of useless information is held each year at the University of Wisconsin's Steven's Point campus. Since 1969, student radio station WWSP 90 FM, the largest of its kind in the Midwest, has held an annual 54-hour trivia marathon. Eight questions are asked each hour, with each correct answer worth 2000 points. Most questions, but not all, are based on an annual theme. In 2006, for example, the theme was "The Odd Contest" based on the film, television series and Broadway show *The Odd Couple.* And not all questions can be answered using the Internet. Thousands of trivia geeks participate each year, and there's even a parade.

GETTING AROUND

No Car Pool Here

Lake Geneva's mail delivery method aside, Wisconsinites like their cars. Driving one's vehicle is by far the most popular method of getting around. There are over four million licensed drivers and 5.3 million registered vehicles in the state. In commuter cities such as Milwaukee, the government tried to encourage energy-saving car pooling by creating "car pool lanes," but the trend never truly caught on. Rather, the car pool lanes remain largely vacant space while the one single-driver lane is clogged with bumper to bumper traffic.

Trains and Planes

For mass transit, Wisconsin has 71 public bus and shared-ride systems, producing a revenue of $73 million annually. Two Amtrak passenger train routes transport about 624,000 passengers per year. There are 134 commercial airports that serve 5400 active aircraft. About 5.5 million travelers fly in or out of Wisconsin each year.

Legwork

Over eight percent of workers choose walking or bicycling as their transportation to work—not many. Again, Wisconsinites like their cars.

The Long and Winding Road
Wisconsin has over 11,000 miles of state and interstate highways. The longest highway is WI 35 at 412.15 miles. It travels from Superior, Wisconsin, to Dubuque, Illinois.

DID YOU KNOW?

Wisconsin was the first state to number its highways.

Staying in the Lines
The roadway known as Interstate 43 is actually an intrastate, because it does not cross Wisconsin state lines.

It's All Connected

Interstates 39, 90 and 94 run concurrently from Madison to Portage, forming the longest distance of concurrent interstate highways in the U.S.

Breaking Trail
Wisconsin has 15,210 miles of snowmobile trails.

Carl Eliason, the inventor of the snowmobile, was from St. Germain, where the International Snowmobile Racing Hall of Fame is currently located.

WISCONSIN'S HEALTH HABITS

Risky Business

According to the 2006 Wisconsin Behavioral Risk Factor Survey, the state's inhabitants are in relatively decent shape. Fifty-eight percent of adults surveyed responded that their overall health was excellent or very good, 30 percent categorized their health as good, and only 12 percent described their health as poor.

The Power of Prevention

While these obligations are no one's idea of a good time, the majority of Wisconsin's older population is taking measures to ensure good health. Seventy-two percent of adults age 65 or older had received a flu shot in the last 12 months, 66 percent of women over 50 had a mammogram, and 64 percent of adults over 50 had a colonoscopy.

Oral Fixation

Seventy-five percent of Wisconsin adults had their teeth cleaned by a dentist or dental technician in 2006. A not-great 39 percent of adults (68 percent of which were 55 years old or older) had lost teeth because of gum disease or decay.

Mental Health

Only 10 percent of adults surveyed had ever been diagnosed with anxiety, while 16 percent had been diagnosed with depression.

DID YOU KNOW?

In 2006, Wisconsin schools received over $4 million in federal money to fund abstinence-until-marriage education programs. Reality check: half of teenage males and females have had sexual intercourse. Sixty-two percent of females and 69 percent of males in Wisconsin reported using a condom.

You Get What You Pay For

According to the federal Agency for Healthcare Research and Quality, the caliber of Wisconsin's health care is the best in the nation. Wisconsin hospitals are rated at the very top, with ambulatory care and nursing-home care also ranking in the top 25 percent. Maybe that explains why most of Wisconsin's health-care costs are as much as 50 percent *higher* than the rest of the Midwest.

Number One Within Number One

The best of the best is Florence, Wisconsin. The University of Wisconsin Health Institute published a 2006 study ranking the state's healthiest counties based on socio-economic factors, physical environment, lifestyle/behaviors and quality of health care. Florence was voted the healthiest. Kudos to Waukesha, Ozaukee, Eau Claire and Portage for rounding out the top five.

Dishonorable Mentions
The least healthy counties listed were Milwaukee, Juneau, Menominee and Adams.

State of Health

Wisconsin was recently ranked the country's 15th healthiest state, according to a study by Morgan Quitno, an independent research publisher. A myriad of criteria were examined, including but not limited to:

☛ Birth weight and infant mortality rate

☛ Immunization percentage

☛ Health insurance coverage: family premiums and percentage of population uninsured

☛ HIV/AIDS rate

☛ STD rate

☛ Obesity rate and exercise habits

☛ Percentage of smokers and heavy drinkers

☛ Estimated rate of new cancer cases

☛ Use of seatbelt percentage

☛ Age-adjusted death rates

We've Got You Covered

In 2005, 89 percent of Wisconsin had health insurance coverage for the full year, 5 percent had insurance for part of the year, and only 5 percent had no insurance. Residents in Wisconsin are more likely to have health insurance coverage than most other states. This is partly because of the Wisconsin government's array of successful programs for the uninsured. About 10 percent of people in the state are covered under SeniorCare, BadgerCare, Healthy Start or Medicaid.

Blood Pressure and Diabetes

Wisconsin is ranked 31st in the country for hypertension, with a rate of 24.5 percent. Even better, a relatively low 6.1 percent of adults suffer from diabetes, ranking Wisconsin 43rd.

The Big C

In 2006, an estimated 26,000 Wisconsin residents were diagnosed with cancer. Generally, 65 percent survive five years beyond the diagnosis, which is right on par with the national average.

While consistent with the rest of the country, it is no less alarming that almost one person in Wisconsin will die of cancer every hour of every day.

Estimated 2006 Wisconsin cancer diagnoses:

☛ Other (27 percent)

☛ Prostate (17 percent)

☛ Female breast (15 percent)

☛ Lung and bronchus (12 percent)

☛ Colon and rectal (10 percent)

☛ Melanoma (5 percent)

☛ Urinary bladder (5 percent)

☛ Leukemia (3 percent)

☛ Non-Hodgkin lymphoma (3 percent)

☛ Uterine (3 percent)

Cause and Effect

Breakdown of approximate estimated causes of cancer:

☛ Tobacco (30 percent)

☛ Diet/obesity (30 percent)

☛ Lack of exercise (5 percent)

☛ Work-related (5 percent)

☛ Family history (5 percent)

☛ Viruses or other biological reasons (5 percent)

☛ Perinatal growth/factors (5 percent)

☛ Reproductive causes (3 percent)

☛ Alcohol (3 percent)

☛ Socio-economic causes (3 percent)

☛ Environmental causes (2 percent)

☛ Ultraviolet radiation (2 percent)

☛ Prescription drugs/medical procedures (1 percent)

☛ Food additives or contaminants (1 percent)

MORBID BITS

Deadly Statistics

☛ There were 46,544 Wisconsin deaths in 2005.

☛ Wisconsin's death rate, currently 8.3 per 1000 people, has been steady with the national death rate since 1945.

☛ In 2005, 72 death certificates indicated work-related injury as the cause of death.

☛ At six percent, Wisconsin's infant mortality rate is lower than the national average. Milwaukee County, however, is the exception, responsible for 31 percent of all infant mortality in the state. And for African Americans in Wisconsin, the infant mortality rate is 19.2 percent, three times the state average.

Cause of Death

The three leading underlying causes of death in Wisconsin are heart disease, cancer and stroke. Approximately 55 percent of all deaths are attributed to those three causes combined.

DID YOU KNOW?

Cremation's hot! The percentage of bodies cremated has steadily increased over the last decade from 20.9 percent in 1996 to 34.1 percent in 2005. The majority of bodies (57.5 percent) are buried, though in 1996, that rate was almost 70 percent. Consistently over the years, 0.6 percent of bodies are donated for medical research or education.

ONE BIG, FAT PROBLEM

Too Much of a Good Thing

All that cheese takes its toll. Wisconsin's current adult obesity rate is 22.9 percent, making it the 28th heaviest state in the country. Wisconsin is hardly well on is way to meeting the national goal to reduce adult obesity to 15 percent by 2010. But in all fairness, no other states have come very close yet, either.

"Cheeseburger Bill" Legislation

Former President Bill Clinton was known to be a fan of the Big Mac, but the Cheeseburger Bill actually refers to the House of Representative's 2004 decision to eliminate weight-gain-based lawsuits. Wisconsin and 23 other states jumped on board with the Personal Responsibility in Food Consumption Act.

Basically, it prohibits litigation-happy citizens (and class-action groups) with a hankering for onion rings and doughnuts from blaming and potentially profiting from food manufacturers, advertisers and restaurants. As Wisconsin Congressman Paul Ryan stated, "Wisconsinites know it isn't right to sue a restaurant simply because of the choices made by its customers."

On the surface, protecting pizzerias and bakeries seems like a crummy way to discourage obesity. The bill's intention is to defend upstanding food businesses, save taxpayer money and instead advocate public health education and individual accountability.

Children Are Our Future

Public health education needs to start early. Over the last 20-plus years, obesity has doubled among children and tripled among adolescents across the country. Blame it on fast food and video games all you want, but eating habits are developed early in life, and if things don't improve, the U.S. is looking at a future adult population with an even greater risk of heart disease, hypertension and certain types of cancer and diabetes.

An Apple a Day Keeps the Nurse Away and Helps You Learn Better!

Wisconsin was one of the first six states to pilot the USDA Fresh Fruit and Vegetable Program. In 2005, $6 million was allocated to each participating state to provide free, healthy snacks to children in 25 elementary and secondary schools per state. Along with improving the eating habits of Wisconsin's youth, it supports the local produce industry. So far, results have been very encouraging. Not enough time has passed to establish its impact on obesity, but by trading in potato chips and soft drinks for carrots and oranges, school administrators are noticing fewer trips to the nurse's office, improved learning abilities and attention spans, and even a decrease in behavior problems. In 2007, nine more states got with the program.

THINGS TO MAKE YOU GO "EWWW"

Mad Cow Disease in Deer!

Chronic wasting disease (CWD) has been likened to mad cow disease because of its effects on the infected animal's nervous system. CWD causes tremors, stumbling and generally strange behavior. It appeared to begin in Canada about 30-plus years ago and was later found in elk and deer in Colorado and then Wyoming. Reports of CWD in Wisconsin deer first popped up in 2002. At least 12 Wisconsin counties have had deer test positive for CWD. Over the last five years, the Wisconsin Department of Natural Resources has taken serious measures to test, control and contain the disease. However, just to be safe and to add to the overall ick-factor, health officials advise hunters to avoid eating the deer parts that tend to harbor the disease—the brain, spinal cord, tonsils, lymph nodes, eyes and spleen. Thanks, it would have otherwise been tempting.

Something to Tick You Off

Like CWD in deer, Wisconsin's extensive wooded and rural areas make the state a prime breeding and feeding ground for ticks that carry Lyme disease. This bacterial infection can be transmitted from ticks to humans. Nothing to sneeze at, this vector-borne illness can afflict different areas of the human body and cause a variety of symptoms and disabilities.

According to the Centers for Disease Control (CDC), Wisconsin has had 13,546 reports of Lyme disease since 2000. That ranks Wisconsin fifth in the country in Lyme disease presence, though the CDC estimates that only one in 10 infections are actually diagnosed and reported. Some studies predict Lyme disease cases will increase by about 33 percent in the next five years.

On a positive note, for 2007, a relatively low 34 cases of Lyme disease had been reported in Wisconsin as of July 7.

Mid-West Nile Virus

Originally confined to Africa, the Middle East and parts of Europe and Asia, West Nile virus (WNV) made its way to the U.S. and first appeared in Wisconsin in 2001. WNV is an arthropod-borne virus in which infected mosquitoes pass the disease onto wild birds and certain mammals such as horses. But when WNV was reported to have infected a Wisconsin human in 2002, it caused quite a stir. Fortunately, the disease never spread too far. So far, 2007 statistics show only seven Wisconsin birds found currently carrying WNV, and no mosquitoes or horses have tested positive. Zero human cases were reported in 2007.

DID YOU KNOW?

Milwaukee wins the prize for having the biggest waterborne outbreak in U.S. history. Is there a trophy for that? In 1993, two cryptosporidium-contaminated water plants led to 403,000 ill residents (with diarrhea, dehydration and other unpleasant symptoms), and even 100 deaths. Eighty miles away, Madison got in on the action when cryptosporidium turned up in Dane County swimming pools.

Nothing to Monkey Around With

A decade after the crypto chaos, Wisconsin became the talk of the infectious disease control community in 2003, when the first person-to-person transmission of the exotic African-based monkeypox disease emerged. In all, over 20 Wisconsin cases of humans infected with the rare virus were reported. The source of the disease was linked to sick prairie dogs, and subsequently, the sale of prairie dogs was banned for a time. It may have put a damper on the annual Prairie Dog Blues Festival in Prairie du Chien that year.

 Scientists in California, France, Italy and other wine-rich regions have been touting the health benefits of a glass of red wine for years. Now Wisconsin can claim that a 24-pack of Leinenkugel's Creamy Dark Lager makes a strong "case" for good health as well. In 2003, University of Wisconsin-Madison professor John D. Folts presented evidence linking dark beer consumption to better heart health. Folts' research, unveiled at the American Heart Association's Scientific Session, demonstrated that antioxidant-abundant flavonoids found in dark beer prevented or reduced blood clots in dogs. Human tests were to follow. Hmm, drinking beer for the good of research and humanity...presumably, Wisconsinites are lining up to volunteer for that study!

EARLY LEARNING

Getting a Good Grade

Wisconsin gets an "A"! When graded on its adequacy of resources for K-12 education, *Education Week* gave Wisconsin a strong "A." Rightfully so—about 45 percent of the state's budget is allocated for education-related expenses.

DID YOU KNOW?

Watertown was the location of the county's first kindergarten back in 1856. Its first students spoke German! Language aside, it quickly became the model for early education across the country.

Teaching Standards

Almost 99 percent of Wisconsin teachers meet the standard to be considered "highly qualified."

Staying in School

Wisconsin's high school graduation rate is the highest in the U.S. at close to 90 percent, compared to the national average of 67 percent. It also has the second lowest drop-out rate in the country, at 2.3 percent.

Smart Stuff

According to Morgan Quitno, an independent research publishing company, Wisconsin is the eighth smartest state. (Their 2004–05 study placed Wisconsin fifth.) The rankings are based on graduation and drop-out rates, pupil-to-teacher ratios and writing and math proficiency, among other indicators.

Salary Woes

Wouldn't recommend coming to Wisconsin to teach right after college, though. Sadly, the average starting salary for new teachers in Wisconsin is just over $25,000 annually, ranking them 49th in the country. Only North Dakota pays worse.

The Proof Is in the Scores

In the pre-college admission ACT exam, Wisconsin students have earned the highest scores almost every year since 1995. They've also scored the third highest SAT results.

DID YOU KNOW?

According to *Expansion Management* magazine, Madison's public schools were ranked eighth in the country in 2006.

It's Never Too Early

Along with debating baby names, following a 20-page instruction booklet on crib assembly and painting a room blue or pink, expectant parents (and grandparents, godparents, aunts and uncles) have one more thing to worry about: college planning. Everyone knows college isn't cheap. To help prepare financially, the Wisconsin Office of the State Treasurer administers a trust-fund-like tax plan called EdVest. It allows Wisconsin residents to make monetary contributions into an account for the beneficiary's post-secondary education, state and federal tax free! (Non-Wisconsin residents can also open an EdVest account, but state taxes may apply.) The earlier you start, the better, so as the child grows, your investments do, too. EdVest has even been gaining popularity on baby shower registries.

HIGHER LEARNING

Lucky 13

The University of Wisconsin system has 13 campuses across the state along with 13 UW-Extension centers. Waukesha County is in the process of proposing an additional UW campus in its neck of the woods.

DID YOU KNOW?

Actor, seven-time Mr. Olympia winner and California Governor Arnold Schwarzenegger graduated from the University of Wisconsin-Superior in 1979 with a Bachelor of Arts degree in international marketing of fitness and business administration.

Being Neighborly

Wisconsin and neighboring Minnesota have a reciprocity agreement dating back to 1968 that allows college students to attend universities in either state and still pay the substantially reduced residential tuition rate.

America's Biggest Party School also Happens to be Wisconsin's Best

UW-Madison consistently heads up the list of *The Princeton Review*'s "Ten Schools that Party the Hardest." It is also one of America's most prestigious state universities (it is frequently named one of the top 10 best public universities) and one of the most difficult Wisconsin colleges to get into—only 22.8 percent of students who applied to the College of Engineering were accepted in fall 2006. Do over 40,000 students a year gravitate to UW to party or to receive an outstanding education? They probably want the best of both worlds.

Is There a Doctor in the House?

UW-Madison has awarded over 30,000 doctorates, almost more than any institution in the world (Harvard is the only U.S. university to exceed them—but they'll give anyone a doctorate, right?). The faculty and alumni of the University of Wisconsin-Madison have received a combined 17 Nobel Prizes and 30 Pulitzer Prizes. It is also widely considered one of the finest biotechnology research centers in the world.

Party Central

The "party school" reputation is not undeserved. UW-Madison is one of the largest binge-drinking campuses in the nation, and the city's downtown State Street is the hub of plenty of student shenanigans—riots after Badger games, a famously wild annual Halloween party (attended by over 100,000 partygoers in 2005, it culminated in 447 arrests and resulted in police donning riot gear and wielding pepper spray for the fourth consecutive year)—and it even took a turn hosting "Weedstock."

More About UW-Madison

Founded in 1848, UW-Madison is a school with long-standing traditions and interesting historical tidbits:

☛ To really ensure that freshmen didn't blend in and to make certain they became targets for ridicule and social exclusion, there was an early dress code that required freshmen to wear green Eton caps.

☛ What was it with caps? After a Badger victory in the 1920s, the UWM marching band started wearing their caps backward. Most likely this was not a gang gesture, though it may have been an attempt to shed the band geek image. Actually, it represented looking back at their win.

☛ As a Homecoming tradition, graduating law students would throw white canes over the goalposts, and if they caught their canes on the other side, they were supposedly destined to win their first case. No word on whether the tossed canes ever hit anyone and resulted in a lawsuit.

☛ It's actually "Buck you!" Enduring mascot Bucky Badger's full name is Buckingham U. Badger. For some reason, that sounds more British than Wisconsinite.

☛ Something's *way* ahead of inflation. In 1900, annual tuition was $20.

- *The Daily Cardinal* was the campus's first student newspaper, published in 1892 (yawn). More excitingly, the witty satire rag, *The Onion* was created by two UW-Madison juniors, Christopher Johnson and Tim Keck, in 1988. Some credit *The Onion* as being a major influence on other news parodies such as Comedy Central's *The Daily Show*.

- UW-Madison has the 15th highest enrollment rate in the country, though that study counted the University of Phoenix (you know, the *online* campus, which really isn't a campus, is it?) since they claim to conveniently "educate" almost three times as many students. So let's just say Wisconsin ranks 14th after all.

- The UW-Madison Badgers are the only Big Ten team to win back-to-back Rose Bowls, in 1999 and 2000. (They also won in 1984.)

DID YOU KNOW?

Renowned writer Joyce Carol Oates earned her Master of Arts degree in English at UW-Madison. It was at a party there that she met Raymond J. Smith. They married in 1961 after three months of dating and are still together.

Joan of Arc Prayed in Marquette

A beautiful oratory named the Chapelle de St. Martin de Sayssuel rested on the French countryside for over 500 years until 1927, when it was purchased by railroad heir Gertrude Hill Gavin. The chapel was dismantled and shipped to her in Long Island piece by piece. Legend claims that in the 15th century, Joan of Arc once prayed on a stone in the original French chapel and, upon finishing, kissed the stone at her feet, which forever after remained colder to the touch than any of the surrounding stones. When Gavin had the chapel reconstructed, she included the Joan of Arc stone. In 1967, the Gavin estate was passed onto Mr. and Mrs. Marc Rojtman, who in turn donated the chapel to Marquette University in Milwaukee. Marquette believes that its Saint Joan of Arc Chapel is "the only medieval structure in the entire Western Hemisphere dedicated to its original purpose."

Golden Eagles

The Marquette Warriors basketball team, coached by the legendary Al Maguire, won their first and only NCAA title in 1977. The team's name has since changed. After a proposal to call them the Marquette Gold was rebuffed, they finally settled on the Marquette Golden Eagles.

DID YOU KNOW?

Twenty-eight percent of Wisconsin's 18- to 24-year-olds from low-income households are enrolled in a higher-education program, ranking Wisconsin 17th in the country. Maybe that explains why so many adults in their 20s are still living at home.

THE GREAT VOUCHER DEBATE

Milwaukee Sets the Precedent

Wisconsin became the first state to run a modern school voucher program when its lawmakers approved the controversial Milwaukee Parental Choice Program (MPCP) in 1989. The program's intention is to allow low-income children to obtain a better education by attending private schools using government dollars. From the get-go, anti-voucher voices argued that state funding could be better spent improving the public schools as opposed to taking a few students out and giving the money to private schools. Oh, and a few Milwaukee residents are probably against the program because almost half of their recent property tax increase is put toward schools just to bankroll voucher students—that's a $7.6 million property tax increase strictly dedicated to the voucher program. Only six other states plus the District of Columbia have dared to follow suit with their own versions of the program.

The Supreme Court Gets Involved

In 1998, the Wisconsin Supreme Court overturned a lower court decision with a 4–2 vote that voucher-recipient schools could include religious schools. At the time, the U.S. Supreme Court declined to review the decision and allowed religious schools to jump in at the state's discretion. However, in 2002, the U.S. Supreme Court weighed in when the issue cropped up again in Ohio. Could religious schools receive government funding by participating as a voucher school? By a close 5–4 vote, the ruling in *Zelman, Superintendent of Public Instruction of Ohio, et al, v. Simmons-Harris et al* declared that religious schools taking voucher students did not violate the Establishment Clause. Since the Establishment Clause applies to the separation of church and state and is interpreted as meaning that the government is not allowed to show preference to or support any particular religion, many were surprised that government dollars going to Catholic, Protestant or Jewish private school tuition was considered constitutional. And it just so happens that Milwaukee's St. Anthony Catholic School has 966 voucher students, the most in the program, making it the highest parochial school recipient of public money ever in the nation.

Taking Advantage of Good Intentions

Scandals! A lot of the criticism of the MPCP is directed at the schools themselves. Over the years, many schools have been cut off from the program for inadequacy, misappropriation, or worse, downright abuse. The Mandella School of Science and Math was not only ordered out of the voucher program, but had to shut down entirely in 2004 when it was revealed that the relatively new "private school" had few books and no real curriculum. Then there was the principal who cashed in $300,000 of voucher money for students that didn't even attend and used the funds to purchase himself two Mercedes-Benz luxury vehicles. Even though some studies show that MPCP students are performing well, when schools such as Mandella close, there is no plan for the displaced students. In 2005, more stringent requirements for schools to qualify as voucher recipients were implemented, such as standardized testing and an accreditation.

Still Going

Despite some mixed results, 2006 saw the second biggest increase in MPCP enrollment in the 17 years of the program's existence. Nearly 18,000 students, or about 24 percent of all public school children, were attending school on vouchers, to the tune of over $100 million. As of 2007, the estimated total cost of vouchers was up to $110 million.

PARTY TIME!

Party Like It's 1899

Defect from Republican to Democrat! That's what many of Wisconsin's German immigrants did at the end of the 19th century when the Bennett Law was proposed. Backed by the Republican Party, the Bennett Law prohibited foreign languages being taught or spoken at American schools. So the Democrat Party gained a wealth of new members, immigrants eager to repeal the law.

Close Calls

Despite the state's Republican roots, a Republican presidential candidate has not prevailed in a Wisconsin election since 1984. But the race has usually been close, and the last couple of elections were downright neck and neck. Even though Wisconsin only controls 11 electoral votes, candidates from both main political parties usually court Wisconsin as a "swing state" ripe for the picking.

Recent election results:

2004:   John Kerry (D)   49.70 percent of
                                the popular vote
        George W. Bush (R)   49.32 percent

2000:   Al Gore (D)   48.38 percent
        George W. Bush (R)   47.87 percent

1996:   Bill Clinton (D)   49 percent
        Bob Dole (R)   38 percent
*Ross Perot accumulated about 10 percent of Wisconsin votes.

1992:   Bill Clinton (D)   41 percent
        George H.W. Bush (R)   37 percent
*Making things really interesting, Perot racked up 21 percent of the votes that year.

1988:	Michael Dukakis (D)	51 percent
	George H.W. Bush (R)	48 percent
1984:	Ronald Reagan (R)	54 percent
	Walter Mondale (D)	45 percent
1980:	Ronald Reagan (R)	48 percent
	Jimmy Carter (D)	43 percent

The Republican Party! In February 1854, a group of freethinkers congregated in Ripon to discuss political reform. Their main platforms of discontent were the practice of slavery and pro-slavery provisions in the Kansas-Nebraska Act. It would be at a meeting in Jackson, Michigan, where the party was first referred to as "Republican." Cities such as Crawfordsville, Iowa, and Exeter, New Hampshire, lay claim to the origins of important Republican beginnings, but Ripon hosted the official foundation of the Republican Party. The Little White Schoolhouse where the meeting took place is listed on the National Register of Historic Places.

DID YOU KNOW?

Governor Bob Doyle was Wisconsin's first Democratic Governor to be reelected in 32 years. It probably helped that his opponent, Mark Green, was involved in allegations that he had used campaign funds illegally.

Voter Turnout, Not Burnout

Wisconsin "rocks the vote." In 2006, 66 percent of Wisconsin residents legally old enough to vote performed their civic duty. It might not sound like an overwhelming turnout, but the national average is less than 50 percent.

PROMINENT POLITICAL FIGURES

Israel's Former Prime Minister

While her political accomplishments may not have affected
Wisconsin specifically, Golda Meir emigrated from Kiev to
Milwaukee in 1906 and went on to have a profound influence
on the *world*. So she deserves a place as a "Prominent Wisconsin
Political Figure." She made effective advances in many posts in
the Israeli government, serving as ambassador to the Soviet
Union, Minister of Labor and National Insurance, Foreign
Minister, Secretary-General of Mapai and then the newly

formed Labor Party. She finally became the world's third female prime minister in 1969. Currently, both a Milwaukee school and the University of Wisconsin-Milwaukee library are named after her.

From Golda Meir to the Golden Fleece

Democratic Wisconsin Senator William Proxmire served five terms in the U.S. Senate and was known for his high energy, integrity and dedication to money conservation. Work ethic personified, he still holds the record for the most consecutive U.S. Senate votes—he attended over 10,000 roll call votes in a row. But his greatest legacy was his crusade to not squander taxpayer money. He practiced what he preached by refusing campaign contributions in his last two elections and declining government funding for traveling abroad. From March 1975 to December 1988, he issued his self-proclaimed Golden Fleece Award to the most "wasteful, ridiculous or ironic use of taxpayers' money." The award is to government programs what the Raspberry Awards are to U.S. cinema. No one was exempt, and Proxmire's Golden Fleece Awards acted as watchdog, encouraging all recipients of government monies to use them responsibly.

Fleecing the Government

According to the Taxpayers for Common Sense Advisory Board, of which Proxmire was named honorary chairman in 1999, the following are the top 10 from Proxmire's era of the Golden Fleece Hall of Shame:

10. Surfing Subsidy

To the 1981 Department of Commerce for giving Honolulu $28,600 for a study evaluating how they could spend another $250,000 for a good surfing beach. At the time, even a few Honolulu officials protested the grant, knowing that local surfers would be available as volunteers. A gnarly abuse of money, dude!

9. Basketball Therapy
To the Health Care Financing Administration for Medicaid payments to psychiatrists for unscheduled and coincidental meetings with patients who were attending basketball games, sitting on stoops or going about their daily business—the cost of which was between $40 million and $80 million from 1981 to 1984. No wonder psych professionals started following patients around and "bumping into them" at the mall and the zoo.

8. $2 Million Patrol Car
To the Law Enforcement Assistance Administration for spending $2 million in 1978 on a prototype police patrol car that was never completed. The car was loaded with gadgets and would have cost $49,078. Please, these vehicles were for beat cops, not James Bond.

7. Tailhook
To the U.S. Navy for using 64 planes to fly 1334 officers to the Hilton Hotel in Las Vegas for a 1974 reunion of the Tailhook Association. There would be worse publicity for Tailhook farther down the road...

6. Tennis Cheaters
To the National Endowment for the Humanities in 1977 for a $25,000 grant to study why people cheat, lie and act rudely on (drumroll, please) public transportation? School property? Nope...local Virginia tennis courts! Actually, if John McEnroe had been available for the study, it might have been productive.

5. TV-Watching Lessons
To the Office of Education for spending $219,592 in 1978 to develop a college curriculum that taught students how to watch television. This was even before the prevalence of those complicated remote controls. Uh, you press "Power" and sit down?

4. New Jersey Sewer Museum
To the Environmental Protection Agency for spending an extra $1 million to $1.2 million in 1980 to preserve a Trenton, New

Jersey, sewer as a historical monument. A sewer! Did they commission artists to create statues of influential rats and other sewer dwellers?

3. How to Buy Worcestershire Sauce
To the U.S. Army for spending $6000 in 1981 to prepare a 17-page document that informed the federal government how to buy a bottle of Worcestershire sauce. This one is truly baffling. Maybe they were trying to concoct an absolutely perfect Bloody Mary.

2. Great Wall of Bedford, Indiana
To the Economic Development Administration of the Commerce Department for spending $20,000 in 1981 to construct an 800-foot-long limestone replica of the Great Wall of China in Bedford, Indiana. And the point of that was…?

1. Tequila Fish
To the National Institute on Alcohol Abuse and Alcoholism for spending millions of dollars in 1975 to find out if drunk fish are more aggressive than sober fish; if young rats are more likely than adult rats to drink booze in order to reduce anxiety; and if rats can be systematically turned into alcoholics. 'Nuff said.

DID YOU  KNOW?

In 2001, Wisconsin Democrat Russ Feingold was the only senator to vote against the Patriot Act. Post 9/11, Congress easily passed the proposal to expand law enforcement's authority to investigate suspected terrorist activity, but Feingold raised concerns that it could infringe on civil liberties.

McCarthy, The Talking Dummy

A Promising Start

Senator Joseph McCarthy came from odd but not entirely unconventional Wisconsin beginnings: teen chicken farm entrepreneur, grocery clerk then manager, Marquette University boxer. Demonstrating relentless ambition and perseverance early on, he was elected president of his law class. Very quickly after earning his law degree, he became the youngest circuit judge ever elected in Wisconsin at the age of 30. After a stint in World War II, he set his sights like a missile target on higher public office. He upset Robert M. LaFollette Jr. for the Republican Senate nomination and became the youngest member of the U.S. Senate.

Taking Things to the Extreme

In a 1950 speech, McCarthy famously accused U.S. Secretary Dean Acheson of having knowledge of 205 State Department Communists. With the Cold War escalating, intense investigations and media hysteria ensued. McCarthy never revealed a shred of credible evidence to back up his charges, mind you, but the mere association of various political, military and entertainment figures with Communism smeared reputations and ruined lives. Many refrained from publicly opposing McCarthy out of fear he would then point his finger at them. CBS Broadcaster Edward R. Murrow was one of the first to condemn McCarthy and his witch hunt on the air, and public opinion started to sway.

But McCarthy had no one but himself to blame for his epic downfall. His performance at the 1954 televised Army-McCarthy Hearings revealed him to be a paranoid, self-righteous and even unstable man. The Senate formed their own committee to investigate McCarthy and voted 67–22 to censure his power. Always a heavy drinker, McCarthy's drinking increased after his denouncement. On May 2, 1957, McCarthy died of hepatitis and is buried at St. Mary's Cemetery in Appleton.

William H. Rehnquist, the Lone Ranger

"Conservative" would be putting it mildly. Milwaukee native Rehnquist was nominated by former President Nixon to be an associate justice and took up the position in January 1972. Early on, he gained his "lone ranger" nickname for being unafraid to speak against all others. He dissented in *Roe v. Wade* and opposed affirmative action. When Chief Justice Warren Burger retired in 1986, Rehnquist took his seat. Over the years, he continued to vote conservatively but also learned to agree with the consensus when appropriate.

Robert M. LaFollette, the Fighter with the Big Idea

In 1900, "Fighting Bob" LaFollette started the first of his three terms as governor of Wisconsin. Known for his outspoken and progressive ideals, he fought for and was successful in implementing greater railroad regulations and new taxation for corporations. These reforms, based on the recommendations of experts in their industries, became known as the "Wisconsin Idea." In 1906, he brought the Wisconsin Idea to Washington when he was elected to the Senate. After several unsuccessful bids for a presidential nomination, he died in 1925. Thirty-two years later, the U.S Senate named LaFollette one of the five greatest senators of all time.

Breaking Barriers

When she was elected in 1998, Madison Democrat Tammy Baldwin became the first non-incumbent openly gay or lesbian member of Congress. She is also the first Wisconsin woman in the House of Representatives and has been reelected four consecutive times. She introduced the Christopher and Dana Reeve Paralysis Act and has been instrumental in progressing legislation to protect farmers, expand hate crime laws, allow stem cell research and advocate for civil rights.

DID YOU KNOW?

Teddy Roosevelt was shot in Wisconsin. At the age of 28, Theodore Roosevelt was the Progressive Party's presidential nominee, and his campaign brought him to Milwaukee on October 14, 1912. As he was leaving the Gilpatrick Hotel, a barkeep named John Schrank shot him in the chest at close range with a .32-caliber bullet. Fortunately, Roosevelt had stowed the case for his trademark glasses in his breast pocket, along with the pages of his evening speech, and they took the force of the blow. He only suffered a flesh wound and, ever the "Rough Rider," delivered his speech before being taken to the hospital. The speech later came to be known as the "Bull Moose Speech," because tough-guy Roosevelt announced to the crowd, "You see, it takes more than one bullet to kill a bull moose."

LEGAL HIGHLIGHTS

Uncommon Law

Dr. John R. Commons (1862–1945) was a University of Wisconsin economics professor who passionately advocated for laws that protected workers without unfairly disrupting the operation of large-scale industry. He firmly believed in the importance of effective labor legislation that favored both employer and employee in a capitalist society. Commons' thinking spurred Wisconsin's most important new labor laws, especially industrial safety and unemployment insurance.

DID YOU KNOW?

Arthur J. Altmeyer, an student of Commons who was strongly influenced by his professor's ideas, became a key figure in the Social Security Act of 1935. President Franklin Roosevelt dubbed Altmeyer "Mr. Social Security."

Wisconsin Firsts

☞ For over 100 years, Wisconsin has been a strong leader in developing positive programs and initiating laws to protect and advance its citizens and workforce. This includes much unprecedented legislation pertaining to wages, work hours, apprenticeships and discrimination.

☞ Wisconsin's first employee safety law, passed in 1887, required fences or other protective guards around machining equipment such as shafts, gears and pulleys.

☞ In 1907, Wisconsin became the first state to offer pensions to blind citizens.

☛ Wisconsin was also the first state to pass a Workmen's Compensation Act in 1911. This law was approved at the U.S. Supreme Court level in 1926.

☛ Ever the employee-friendly state, Wisconsin was a pioneer in offering unemployment insurance, starting in 1932. Three years later, the U.S. Social Security Act would adopt unemployment rights nationwide. The first unemployment compensation check was issued in the amount of $15; the recipient sold the check for its historical significance to Paul Rauschenbush, who served as the Director of the Unemployment Compensation Division from 1932 to 1967, for $25. The check is currently displayed at the Wisconsin State Historical Society. Wisconsin was also the first state to implement an interactive and automated telephone system for reporting and processing unemployment claims.

☛ In 1945, Wisconsin became one of the first three states to invoke the Fair Employment Law, prohibiting employment discrimination on the basis of race, creed, color or national origin.

☛ To organize state services and housing and employment resources for refugees, Wisconsin created the nation's first Office of Refugee Services in 1975.

DID YOU KNOW?

When Wisconsin became the 30th state to enter the Union, its voting laws were among the most liberal around. Its constitution allowed aliens the right to vote if they had resided in the state for at least a year and declared their intention to become citizens. Ever the trendsetter, other states soon followed suit.

The Vanna White Veto

While any governor has the authority to just say no to any bill, Wisconsin's governor is entitled to more power than most when it comes to the veto. It is not unusual for states to offer "line-item" veto power, which allows a governor to reject a proposal or strike particular components. About a dozen states also grant "reduction" veto power, permitting the governor to restrict expenditures on a bill. A handful of governors enjoy "amenda-tory" veto control, which enables them to rewrite legislature. Wisconsin uniquely allows all three loopholes: line-item, reduc-tion and amendatory vetoes! Governor Doyle took advantage of that in 2005, when he removed 752 words from a budget bill so that the remaining verbiage reallocated $427 million from transportation to education. Since a two-thirds majority of his legislature did not override his creative veto, the bill passed. Critics referred to Doyle's tactic as the "Vanna White" veto, inspired by the *Wheel of Fortune* hostess who turned letters around.

Who Votes for Skipping the Exam?

Wisconsin's two law schools, the University of Wisconsin and Marquette University, abide by the "diploma privilege," a 134-year-old rule that exempts law school graduates from taking the bar exam so they can practice law. The intention is for law stu-dents to spend less time focusing on studying for the bar and more time studying a broad spectrum of cases. The majority of Wisconsin's 21,000-plus licensed attorneys have never taken the bar exam. Beneficiaries of the diploma privilege include Attorney General Peg Lautenschlager, Milwaukee mayor Tom Barrett and six of the seven state Supreme Court justices. Other states had similar provisions, but since West Virginia changed their policy in 1988, Wisconsin is the last remaining state.

Free makeup samples at the cosmetics counter. Free fruit samples at the farmer's market. Why not free beer? A bill to allow grocers and liquor stores to offer persons of legal drinking age up to 6 ounces of free beer samples is gaining steam. Both beer-loving chambers of legislature unanimously voted yes to the idea.

The Demise of the Death Penalty

The former home of John and Bridget McCaffrey at 13 Court Street is a registered historical landmark because of the significance of Mr. McCaffrey's death. Now, John McCaffrey was no martyr—and he had a bit of a temper. He was found guilty of murdering his wife by beating, choking and eventually shoving her body into a barrel until she finally died from drowning, and Judge E.V. Whiton sentenced McCaffrey to death by execution. When his fateful day arrived on August 21, 1851, McCaffrey was paraded in front of the townspeople and officials, and then blindfolded and hooded. Then nothing. At least not for five whole minutes, as the sheriff waited for the clock to reach the 1:00 PM execution time ordered by the governor. The crowd waited on the edges of their seats. Finally, tripping on the way, the sheriff walked to the platform, and McCaffrey was hanged. For over five minutes, his dangling body squirmed, and he was still alive 10 long minutes after that. Some might say that kind of torturous execution was fitting, considering his wife died from slowly drowning in inches of murky barrel water. Most were horrified. The execution was finally, um, successful, but the public was outraged. The editor of the *Kenosha Telegraph*, C. Latham Sholes, wrote, "We hope this will be the last execution that shall ever disgrace the mercy-expecting citizens of the State of Wisconsin." Two years later, the Death Penalty Repeal was signed by Governor Farwell, and Wisconsin has not executed anyone since. Wisconsin has prohibited the death penalty for 154 years, longer than any other state.

WISCONSIN LAW: WISE AND OTHERWISE

Butter is better. The Surgeon General might disagree, but in 1925, Wisconsin lawmakers were adamant. In fact, they passed a law declaring it illegal to manufacture or sell margarine in Wisconsin. Its attempt to support the dairy industry was overruled in 1927 in *John F. Jelke Company v. Emery.*

You Go, Girl!

☛ Wisconsin helped advance women's rights with a couple of pivotal cases. In 1875, Janesville lawyer Lavinia Goodell was the first woman to apply for admission to the bar of the Wisconsin Supreme Court. Her application was rejected. Following legislation that prohibited denying admittance to the bar based on gender, she reapplied two years later and succeeded.

☛ Wisconsin became the first state to ratify the national women's suffrage amendment. In 1919, suffrage advocate Ada James' father, Senator David G. James, delivered the documents to Washington, DC.

☛ In 1926, the Wisconsin Supreme Court ruled 4–3 that women should have the right to sue their husbands. One can only guess that the three dissenters were not in the most blissful of marriages.

DID YOU KNOW?

In Wisconsin, if an unmarried or widowed parent dies, the adult children are not legally free to sue for malpractice. Similarly, parents are unable to sue for malpractice if their child over the age of 18 dies. Only six other states abide by these malpractice limitations.

I Wouldn't Touch that Copy of
Tropic of Capricorn

Next time you check out *Mein Kampf, How to Build a Bomb* or the latest *Gossip Girl* guilty pleasure, rest assured that your identity remains confidential—even if you choose to gratify yourself on the spot in the Neenah Public Library, as a man allegedly did in 2007! One could only assume (or at least hope) that he wasn't aware that it was all being captured on surveillance video. Well, that footage was the only thing captured in this case. Claiming it is legally obligated to protect the overzealous library user's identity, the library is refusing to turn the incriminating video over to the police without a court order. Which sends a disturbing message that you can commit a crime and get away with it—just do it in a library!

And You Thought Women Were Obsessed with Shoes

Call him the Locker Room Bandit or the Keds Klepto. In 2007, 26-year-old Erich Heinrich was arrested in Waukesha for stealing over 1500 pairs of used gym shoes. Apparently, Heinrich used his job at a cable company to gain access to at least five middle and high schools, where he would raid the girls' locker rooms and make off with dirty sneakers. Eww!

TRUE CRIME

Safe Cities

According to Morgan Quitno Press, an independent research company that ranks states and cities in various categories, Wisconsin boasts an impressive six of the top 10 safest metropolitan areas in the United States in 2006: Fond du Lac (1st), Eau Claire (4th), Appleton (5th), Sheboygan (6th), La Crosse (8th) and Wausau (10th). Oshkosh-Neenah just missed the top 10 by coming in 12th. Rock on!

Murderous Decline

In 2006, there were 166 reported murders in Wisconsin, down 19.8 percent from a body count of 207 in the previous year. Conversely, the number of arrests for murder crimes went up in 2006. Adult murder arrests went up 9.3 percent, while juvenile arrests went up a remarkable 69.2 percent. Take that, criminals!

Aggravating Assaults

Reports of aggravated assault, however, rose 21.6 percent, with 9347 reported incidents in 2006.

Robbed!

Lock your doors. Property-based offenses were up across the board, with 27,135 burglaries committed, 13,507 cars stolen and a staggering 116,389 reports of theft in 2006.

A Dangerous Age

Definitely nothing to brag about, but Wisconsin has more homicides in which the victims are teens than any other state (8 percent).

Long Odds

If you lived in Wisconsin in 2005, the odds of being a victim of a violent crime were one in 410, compared to the rest of the Midwest, where odds were 242 to one, and nationwide, with odds of 213 to one.

Less Violent Crime

All in all, the rate of violent crime in Wisconsin is 30 percent lower than the rest of the Midwest and 18 percent lower than the United States average.

Gangstas...

Like most of the country, Wisconsin has a serious problem with gangs, and the trend seems to be evolving and spreading. It is no longer simply the large cities that are experiencing gang activity. Nationwide, the most recent study claims the average population of a city with gang activity decreased from 182,000 people to just 34,000. The Crips, Kings and Disciples are heading for the hills. Over the last decade, the Midwest has had the second largest increase (the South being first) in newly reported gang territories. Wisconsin, in particular, ranked 17th nationally in the infiltration of gang presence into previously gang-free areas. Over half of its counties citied first-time reports of gangs. Law enforcement officials attribute this to expanded drug-trade venues and minority immigrants settling in rural areas. Common opinion likes to blame Chicago.

...and Gangsters

Al Capone

Wisconsin also had a few encounters with notorious gangsters in another era. Al Capone, "Public Enemy Number One" of his day, spent time in a lakefront Couderay vacation home. Sprawling 400 acres along the Chippewa Flowage, this retreat was an ideal sanctuary for hiding-out. It had 18-inch-thick, bulletproof walls, a secret bunkhouse, a guard tower equipped with machine guns and a special bedroom switch that simultaneously turned on all the lights in the house.

JOHN DILLINGER

Another FBI Public Enemy Number One, bank robber John Dillinger spent some time in Wisconsin as well. On November 23, 1933, Dillinger and his gang robbed the American Bank & Trust Co. in Racine. Two people were wounded and another three taken hostage. The robbers made away with $27,000. Never one to linger in one place too long, Dillinger pillaged neighboring states, even heading briefly out West. He was captured but escaped from an Indiana jail in 1934, and then he returned to Wisconsin for what would ultimately become a very memorable showdown with the FBI and an embarrassing fiasco for J. Edgar Hoover.

On the run, Dillinger and his gang, including "Baby Face" Nelson, decided to lay low in northern Wisconsin and checked into a quiet resort called Little Bohemia. The lodge owners, Emil Wanatka and his wife, Nan, figured out who their guests were and tipped off the FBI. The cavalry arrived at the nearest airport in Rhinelander and formulated their plan to surround Little Bohemia and, finally, in theory, apprehend or kill Dillinger. Their plan went unpredictably awry. Talk about the wrong place at the wrong time—three innocent patrons were leaving the lodge and getting into a car when the overly trigger-zealous FBI, spurred by J. Edgar Hoover's obsession to catch the elusive Dillinger, opened fire. After a sloppy shootout, two innocent men were dead and the third wounded, plus one law enforcement agent was killed and two more injured. Dillinger, or the "Jackrabbit" as he was fittingly nicknamed, escaped again!

DID YOU KNOW?

Because of abnormalities in Dillinger's autopsy, people who idealized his Robin Hood–inspired thievery disputed that he had, in fact, died. The official report claims he was finally found and subsequently shot to death while leaving the Biograph Theater in Chicago on July 22, 1934. But Chicago writer Jay Robert

Nash pointed out several discrepancies such as the autopsied body showing evidence of a childhood disease Dillinger never had, a heart condition that his prison physician denied he had and the lack of scars that he was known to have had. Perhaps Dillinger is indeed still alive and hiding out in Antarctica along with Elvis, Jim Morrison and Tupac.

Serial Slayers

Even though folks in Elderton eat goat testicles and call it a festival, there is a serious line that can be crossed. Eating or otherwise dismembering human beings goes way over that line. For some reason, a couple of unimaginably disturbed serial killers came from Wisconsin—most notably Edward Theodore Gein and Jeffrey Lionel Dahmer.

ED GEIN

Gein was born in La Crosse in 1906 (despite La Crosse's recent ranking as the eighth safest metropolitan area in America). While only two murders at the hands of Gein were ever proven, he was suspected of several more. His notoriety derived mostly from the bizarre and repulsive manner in which he handled their remains, not the number of victims. Suffice it to say that window blinds, cereal bowls and other typical household goods found in his home were fashioned out of human skins, skulls and other body parts.

JEFFREY DAHMER

Another criminal accused of gruesome acts of necrophilia, cannibalism and creating body-part souvenirs, Milwaukee's Jeffrey Dahmer killed at least 17 victims in his heyday from 1978 to 1991. He never lived to serve his 15 life terms in the Columbia Correctional Institution in Portage. In November 1994, Christopher Scarver, a fellow inmate with a history of having a nasty temper, beat Dahmer severely while the two were on work-detail assignment in the prison gym. Dahmer died on his way to the hospital.

FOR THE EYES

Prairie Houses, Usonian Houses and Lots of Drama

Born in Richland Center and raised in Madison, Frank Lloyd Wright (1867–1959) was a world-renowned architect, though much his best work can be found in his home state. The S.C. Johnson Wax building and Wingspread, both built in Racine in 1938, are two prime examples of his innovative designs and penchant for curves. Both are open to the public for tours.

Wright's organic architecture style established him as the frequently cited greatest and most influential American architect of all time. While his work was widely praised, his personal life became fodder for controversy. While designing a residence for a neighbor, Wright fell in love with the man's wife, Mamah Borthwick Cheney. Even though Wright and Mamah were both married, they scandalously eloped to Europe in 1909. Upon returning to the States a year later, the couple settled in Spring Green, where Wright began work on Taliesin, his new home. He would rebuild and remodel Taliesin many times over the next several decades. One of those occasions was the result of tragic events that happened in the summer of 1914. While Wright was out of town, a servant named Julian Carlton took an ax and killed Mamah, her two children and four workers! He also started a fire that caused considerable damage to the living quarters of Taliesin.

That would be the first of two fires that Wright and Taliesin would endure. Back on the personal front, Wright finally divorced his first wife in 1922, and the next year he married Maude "Miriam" Noel. Because of Miriam's morphine addiction, however, the marriage lasted less than a year. While separated from Miriam, Wright met and fell in love with Olga (Olgivanna) Lazovich Hinzenburg. As Olga's husband tried to obtain custody of his daughter from her, Wright and Olgivanna were arrested for violation of the Mann Act, which addressed prostitution and immorality, though the charges were later dropped. Wright and Olgivanna married in 1928.

DID YOU  KNOW?

Chuck Berry, Charlie Chaplin and Charles Manson were all also prosecuted under the Mann Act.

 One of Wright's later accomplishments, the Seth Peterson Cottage in Lake Delton, had become rundown and abandoned by the 1980s. It was discovered by a woman named Audrey Laatsch, who happened to be canoeing on Mirror Lake. Talk about a hidden gem! She lobbied diligently and succeeded in having the beautiful property restored.

DID YOU  KNOW?

The United Arts Fund ranked Milwaukee number one for donations to the arts per capita.

A Work of Art to House Works of Art

The Milwaukee Art Museum (MAM) earned the honor of *Time* magazine's "Best Design of 2001" when it underwent a major renovation. One of the highlights was the addition of the breathtaking 142,050-square-foot Quadracci Pavilion, the first American building designed by Spanish architect Santiago Calatrava. The Pavilion boasts the Burke Brise Soleil—"wings" that actually move to shield the glass-enclosed Windhover Hall from the sun. Other state-of-the-art features include radiant heating beneath the marble floor and a 280-foot-long pedestrian suspension bridge supported by 3300 locked coil cables.

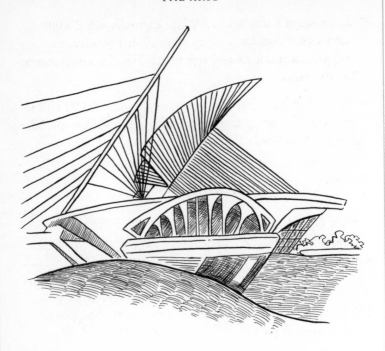

Other facts about the Milwaukee Art Museum:

☛ The museum, called the Milwaukee Art Center until 1980, was formed by the merger of two separate entities, the Layton Art Gallery and the Milwaukee Art Institute, in 1957.

☛ Santiago Calatrava was selected to helm the expansion in 1994. It would take eight years to complete. Since then, he has designed some of the most beautiful structures in the world: the Valencia Opera House in Spain, the Athens Olympic Sports Complex in Greece, Quatro Ponte sul Canal Grande in Venice, Italy, the Tenerife Opera House in Santa Cruz, Canary Islands, and the Blackhall Place Bridge in Dublin, Ireland, to name a few.

☛ The Brise Soleil is taller than the Leaning Tower of Pisa and has a wingspan wider than that of a Boeing 747.

- To construct Calatrava's addition, approximately 20,000 cubic feet of concrete were used. If all that concrete was melded into a one-foot-by-one-foot column, it would extend for 102 miles!

- In the 1990s, the museum averaged almost 200,000 visitors per year. The first year after the renovation was completed, the MAM saw over half a million visitors.

DID YOU  KNOW?

Georgia O'Keefe, a famous painter born to dairy farmers in Sun Prairie and a formidable presence at the MAM, was just as passionate about nature in person as in her paintings. Once, while hiking in a canyon in New Mexico and enthralled by its beauty, she threw her head back and shamelessly howled like a coyote. This gave her nearby friends quite a scare—they thought she was screaming in pain!

FOR THE EARS

Cheeseheads With Attitude

The musical trio known as C.W.A. (Cheeseheads with Attitude) has gained a cult following in Wisconsin for their catchy cover songs with a twist and diehard Packers pride. Their first album, *Straight Outta Wisconsin,* was released in 1996. It includes such Wisconsin-themed songs as "Where the Hell is Neenah?" (to the tune of Tone-Loc's "Funky Called Medina"*)* and their signature lyrics for "Cheesehead Baby" (to the tune of Beck's "Loser"). Follow-up albums such as *Cheeseheads for Life* may not have packed the same novelty but could be construed as entertaining, nonetheless. At least good enough to throw in while you're driving up to Lambeau Field.

Some of the musicians and bands to emerge from the Dairy State include Garbage, the BoDeans, the Steve Miller Band, the Gufs, Citizen King and the Violent Femmes.

And Elton John's Not Gay, Either

West Allis native Wladziu Valentino Liberace, known as Liberace, may be remembered for two things: his talent on the piano and for being one of the gay-est figures of the 20th century. In 1957, he sued the British publication *The Daily Mirror* for libel for implying that he was homosexual. He won the lawsuit after testifying in a London court that he had never participated in homosexual acts nor was he a homosexual.

Decades later, Liberace's live-in boyfriend of five years, Scott Thorson, sued the pianist for $113 million in palimony after their nasty breakup. In the end, Thorson received a $95,000 settlement. Liberace continued to publicly insist that he was not gay.

Liberace's career endured its ups and downs, including a deep slump in the 1970s. Paving the way for David Cassidy and David Hasselhoff, Liberace resurrected a stalled career by making a splash in Las Vegas. The response was enormously positive, and he was able to indulge in sequins and jewels galore.

DID YOU KNOW?

The "King" himself, Elvis Presley, once promoted his evening performance at Milwaukee's Riverside Theater from the back of a truck on Wisconsin Avenue.

LIGHTS, CAMERA, WISCONSIN!

That Wisconsin Show

Who knew so much pot was toked in Wisconsin? For eight seasons, fans of *That '70s Show* followed the adventures of Eric Forman and friends in the fictional town (Kenosha vicinity) of Point Place, Wisconsin. The show made stars of Ashton Kutcher, Topher Grace and, arguably, Wilmer Valderrama. Only one cast member was actually from Wisconsin—tough-love papa Reginald "Red" Forman was played by Kurtwood Smith, who was born on July 3, 1943 in New Lisbon. Smith's extensive stage, television and screen career includes memorable roles in Gus Van Sant's *To Die For,* Woody Allen's *Shadows and Fog,* Joel Schumacher's *A Time to Kill,* Peter Weir's *Dead Poet's Society,* and even a small part in *Staying Alive* with John Travolta.

DID YOU KNOW?

Both Woody Allen's iconic fictional character, Annie Hall, and Leonardo DiCaprio's *Titanic* character, Jack Dawson, claim Chippewa Falls, Wisconsin, as their hometown.

Orson Welles: Citizen Kenosha

Born on May 6, 1915, in Kenosha, Welles is best know for writing, directing, producing and acting in *Citizen Kane,* the 1941 film ranked by the American Film Institute as the best movie of all time. Other facts about the notorious auteur/actor/voice artist:

☛ Welles became infamous for a 1938 Halloween hoax in which he broadcast H.G. Wells' *War of the Worlds* over the radio in news bulletin format. Many listeners believed that Martians were actually invading Earth! Widespread panic ensued.

☛ His acting résumé boasts over 100 credits, but many roles were simply narration or vocal gigs that highlighted his distinctive voice.

☛ George Lucas originally wanted Welles to portray the voice of Darth Vader in *Star Wars.*

☛ He was married to screen siren Rita Hayworth from 1943 to 1948. They produced a daughter, Rebecca.

☛ A Civil Rights advocate, Welles devoted much of his ABC radio show *Orson Welles Commentaries* to support Isaac Woodard. Woodard, an African American World War II veteran, had been forcibly removed from a South Carolina bus without cause by police and beaten in an alley. He was arrested for disorderly conduct, then viciously and permanently blinded. Welles crusaded for Woodard's attackers to be punished, and *Orson Welles Commentaries* was subsequently canceled. Throughout the South, Welles was hanged in effigy.

☛ He also took part in some less-prestigious projects. He appeared in *The Muppet Movie* and a string of commercials for the Paul Masson wine company, and loaned his voice to *Magnum P.I.* His final voice role was in the 1986 animated film *The Transformers: The Movie*, which was released after his death in 1985.

"Look at This #@*%-ing Guy"

Wild thang! Charlie Sheen and crew spent time in Milwaukee during the shooting of *Major League*. Most of the "Cleveland Indians" home game scenes were filmed at Milwaukee's County Stadium with Brewers fans in the stands. Bob Uecker, a Hall of Fame Brewers radio announcer and former Milwaukee Braves player, had a part as announcer Harry Doyle in the movie.

How a Low-Budget Horror Movie Can Make You a Quasi-Celeb

Chris Smith's *American Movie* (1999), set in Milwaukee, can show you more about quintessential Wisconsin than any book (not that you shouldn't still read *this* book!). Mark Borchardt, accompanied by his right-hand man and faithful, perpetually beer-drinking sidekick Mike Schank, was just like any struggling wannabe filmmaker. The difference is that his struggles became material for a hilarious documentary called *American Movie*. As Borchardt tries to write, film and edit his labor of love—a cheap, cheesy, forgettable horror flick called *The Coven*—Smith documents the many obstacles he runs into, the interactions with his family members (all "playing" themselves) and catches some truly choice, seemingly off-the-cuff, quotable one-liners. Although *The Coven* was never exactly a hit, *American Movie* became a cult classic. It even launched Borchardt into quasi-stardom. He was said to be a favorite guest of David Letterman and became a revered fixture for a while at local bars.

Another Semi-Celebrity

MTV's phenomenally popular *Real World* show's Boston cast featured token virgin "Elka," token angry black male "Syrus" and token lesbian "Genesis." It also introduced "Sean," whose character was the wide-eyed country bumpkin and young hormonal male looking for fun. In the actual real world, Sean Duffy was raised along with 10 brothers and sisters in Hayward.

Hayward is the site of the Lumberjack World Championships, and Sean was a three-time champion in the speed climb competition—meaning that he can scale a 90-foot pole like a squirrel scampering up a tree with its tail on fire. Sean was a fine ax thrower as well, though one of Sean's many older brothers, Brian, dominated the slippery lumberjack logrolling category. Sean went on to marry *Real World: San Francisco*'s Rachel Campos and earned another title—the first marital union of two *Real World* alumni. Subsequently, Rachel filled in a couple of times as co-host on *The View,* long before Star Jones lost two-thirds of her body mass and Rosie O'Donnell lost all of her marbles, friends and tact. Sealing his semi-celebrity stature, Sean scored an ESPN commentator gig at the 2003 Great Outdoor Games, where he also competed. The devout Catholic and Republican duo settled in Ashland, where apparently a lot of *Real World* fans (or Republicans) reside, because Sean was elected district attorney in 2004 and even contemplated running for Congress. His popularity continued during the 2004 Winter Games, when Sean was chosen as a Badger State Games Honorary Athlete and given the duty of carrying the torch to the cauldron. Maybe "Puck" and his messenger bike weren't free that day.

Hey, That's the Street Where I Grew Up!

Other movies filmed, in part or whole, in Wisconsin:

Back to School (1986): Madison

The Blues Brothers (1980): Milwaukee

Chain Reaction (1996): Madison

The Deep End of the Ocean (1999): Madison

For Keeps? (1988): Madison

Hoop Dreams (1994): Milwaukee

I Love Trouble (1994): Baraboo and Madison

Meet the Applegates (1991): Neenah and Oshkosh

Milwaukee, Minnesota (2003): Milwaukee, of course!

Mr. 3000 (2004): Milwaukee (Miller Park)

Mrs. Soffel (1984): Freedom

Novocaine (2001): Cedarburg

One Night Stand (1997): Milwaukee

The Paint Job (1992): Milwaukee, Kenosha and Racine

A Simple Plan (1998): Ashland

The Straight Story (1999): Mount Zion and Prairie du Chien

Uncle Buck (1989): Lake Geneva

Hotties that Hail from our Great State
Heather Graham! Born January 29, 1970, she spent her young nights boogying in Milwaukee. Her career was launched in the 1988 Corey Haim/Corey Feldman teen vehicle *License to Drive.* Unlike the Coreys, she went on to find success in both television (recurring roles on *Twin Peaks* and *Scrubs)* and film (*Boogie Nights)* and has crossed back and forth between mainstream (*Austin Powers: The Spy who Shagged Me, Bowfinger*) and independent (*Swingers, Drugstore Cowboy*) films.

Umm, Chris Noth? Born November 13, 1954, in Madison. Some considered him hot as the ultimate self-absorbed, toxic bachelor Mr. Big on *Sex and the City.*

Hmmm…this is really a struggle here…

Well, maybe Wisconsin is not the "Land of the Beautiful People." So the people here must have really phenomenal personalities!

They'll Make Your Sides Hurt

Wisconsin has produced a few seriously funny talents:

Chris Farley: Born February 15, 1964, in Madison. Beloved star of *Saturday Night Live* and *Tommy Boy,* fans were shocked and saddened by his untimely death at the age of 33.

Gene Wilder: Born June 13, 1933, in Milwaukee. The renowned actor-writer-director garnered Oscar nominations for *The Producers* and *Young Frankenstein.* Fan favorites include *Blazing Saddles* and *Willy Wonka and the Chocolate Factory.*

Jackie Mason: Born June 9, 1931, in Sheboygan. His one-man show *The World According to Me* earned him Tony, Emmy, Grammy, Ace Cable and Outer Critic's Circle Awards.

David and Jerry Zucker: Born October 16, 1947, and March 11, 1950, respectively, in Milwaukee. The brothers wrote and directed *Airplane* and *The Naked Gun: From the Files of Police Squad.*

Jane Kaczmarek: Born December 21, 1955, in Milwaukee. She was nominated for eight Emmy Awards for her role as the matriarch on *Malcolm in the Middle.* She is married and has two children with fellow Wisconsin actor, Bradley Whitford, from *The West Wing.*

DID YOU KNOW?

As a probable "wink, wink" to his home state, Bradley Whitford's character on *The West Wing,* Josh Lyman, teased his assistant Donna Moss, whose parents once visited the White House from Wisconsin, by making reoccurring cheese-joke references.

Other Notable Thespians

Don Ameche: Born May 31, 1908, in Kenosha. He starred in *Cocoon* and *Trading Places* as well as many other films from the 1930s until his death in 1993.

Willem Dafoe: Born July 22, 1955, in Appleton. He had roles in *Spider-Man, Mississippi Burning* and *The English Patient*, among others. Commenting on the dark, eccentric roles he often plays in films, he once said, "Weirdness is not my game. I'm just a square from Wisconsin."

Tyne Daly: Born February 21, 1946, in Madison. She is best known for her roles in TV series such as *Cagney and Lacey* and *Judging Amy*.

Deidre Hall: Born October 31, 1947, in Milwaukee. Though she has appeared in other television dramas, she is most familiar as Dr. Marlena Evans Brady Black on *Days of Our Lives*.

Charlotte Rae: Born April 22, 1926, in Milwaukee. An actress since the 1950s, she has appeared in TV series such as *Diff'rent Strokes* and *The Facts of Life*.

Gena Rowlands: Born June 19, 1930, in Madison. The daughter of state legislator E.M. Rowlands, this legendary actress has appeared in nearly 100 films and TV series, including *A Woman Under the Influence* and *Gloria*.

Mark Ruffalo: Born November 22, 1967, in Kenosha. His films include *Eternal Sunshine of the Spotless Mind, Zodiac* and *13 Going on 30*.

Tony Shalhoub: Born October 9, 1953, in Green Bay. Though he had acted in many films for the big screen, his breakout role was that of obsessive-compulsive detective Adrian Monk in the TV series *Monk*.

Spencer Tracy: Born April 5, 1900, in Milwaukee. Known as much for his romance with Katharine Hepburn as for his films, he appeared in *Father of the Bride* and *Guess Who's Coming to Dinner*, to name just a few.

DID YOU KNOW?

For a state with four seasons (winter, winter, winter and road construction), Wisconsin has an unexpected three outdoor theaters: Spring Green's American Players Theatre, Fish Creek's Peninsula Players Theatre and the Lake Superior Big Top Chautauqua.

Not the Rock Band

"I went to school in Wisconsin and I used to drive to see Steppenwolf in a basement."

– Campbell Scott, son of actors George C. Scott and Colleen Dewhurst

In 1983, Campbell Scott graduated in Theatre and Performing Arts (Drama) from Lawrence University in Appleton. One can presume he was referring to the famed Chicago underground Steppenwolf Theatre Company, co-founded by Gary Sinise, rather than the "Magic Carpet Ride" rock group.

MORE ENTERTAINERS

Those with Coulrophobia (Fear of Clowns) Should Skip This One

The Circus World Museum in Baraboo, opened in 1959, is a large complex that hosts circus acts and performances, sponsors the annual Great Circus Parade and preserves the largest archive of circus material and artifacts in the world. It is located near historic Ringlingville, which was the site of the first Ringling Brothers Circus in 1884 and continued to serve as their headquarters and winter grounds until 1917. The U.S. Department of the Interior designated the original Ringling Brothers winter ground buildings as a National Historic Landmark.

Harry Houdini: Debunking the Myths

MYTH: Harry Houdini, the great magician and escape artist, was born in Appleton on April 6, 1874.

TRUTH: Houdini, born Ehrich Weiss on March 24, 1874, was actually from Budapest, Hungary. His family moved to Appleton when he was very young.

MYTH: Houdini had supernatural abilities and could communicate with the dead.

TRUTH: Houdini had an interest in contacting the "other side," propelled by his grief over his mother's death. But after extensive research and frustration, he concluded that it was not possible. He deemed all fortune-tellers as phonies, much like the imitators that sought to steal his tricks, and Houdini made it his mission to expose the frauds. After his own death, his widow attended annual séances for 10 years. No true contact has ever been proven, but the séances continue to this day.

MYTH: Houdini's brother, Theo (performance name Hardeen), burned all of Houdini's magic equipment and notes after his death.

TRUTH: In the event of his death, Houdini had instructed Theo to destroy his tricks. Instead, Theo passed them on to his own protégé, Sidney Radner. Radner stored everything for 40 years before allowing the Outagamie County Historical Society to exhibit them to the public for the first time in 1989.

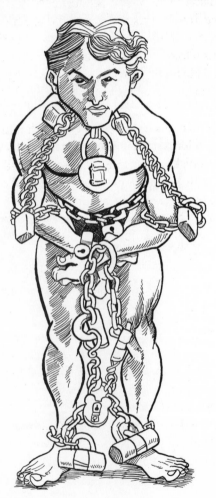

MYTH: Houdini, confident his body could withstand not only straitjackets and other confinement, but also serious physical blows, routinely challenged fans to hit him in the gut as hard as they could. A Canadian college student punched him before he was adequately prepared, and he died of a ruptured appendix.

MYTH: Houdini died during one of his shows when he was unable to escape from an underwater trick and drowned.

TRUTH: The latter myth was perpetrated by a 1953 Houdini biopic starring Tony Curtis that depicted that fictional scenario. The other myth is closer to the truth, because Houdini did die of appendicitis. However, it was caused by a bacterial infection, not a fan's fist. He finally crossed over to the "other side" on Halloween 1926 at Grace Hospital in Michigan.

MYTH: Houdini's name was inspired by French illusionist Jean Eugene Robert-Houdin, and he was responsible for coining Buster Keaton's nickname. Stories claim that Houdini was sharing the stage with Keaton's vaudeville parents and commented after a very young Keaton survived unharmed from a tumble down the stairs, "What a buster your kid took!"

TRUTH: Actually, those two tidbits are true!

SOMETIMES WE READ AND WRITE, TOO

Laura's *Little House*

Laura Ingalls Wilder published her first book in 1932. It was called *Little House in the Big Woods* and was based on her life in her family's cabin in Pepin, where she was born.

DID YOU  KNOW?

Thornton Wilder, born in Madison in 1897, was a Pulitzer Prize–winning author and playwright. No relation to Laura Ingalls Wilder!

Something James Frey Is Never Likely to Achieve

Jane Hamilton, who lives in Rochester, Wisconsin, has penned three books that were recognized by Oprah Winfrey's bestseller-guaranteeing Book Club: *The Book of Ruth* (Hamilton's debut novel, which also received the 1989 PEN/Hemingway Award), *A Map of the World* (named one of the Top Ten Books of 1994 by *Publishers Weekly, People* magazine and *Entertainment Weekly* and adapted into a film in 2000 starring Sigourney Weaver) and, most recently, *Disobedience*. If it's good enough for Oprah…

ENVIRONMENTAL SCIENCE

Not the Environment's Best Friend

With Al Gore and Leonardo DiCaprio bringing global warming and environmental concerns to the mainstream forefront, Wisconsin—a state known for its love of the outdoors—is lagging behind.

Wisconsin was formed by melting glaciers and appears to be experiencing further shifting. Over the last century, the average temperature has only increased by 0.7 degrees, but there has been a noticeable change or homogenization of the seasons. The lines between winter, spring, summer and fall are blurring. Birds that fly south for the winter are coming back sooner, and flowers that bloom in the spring are blossoming earlier.

Hot Topic

Heat stress affecting cattle already costs Wisconsin farmers $60 million a year, and global warming will only worsen it. Maybe Wisconsinites will be inspired to go greener when they realize quality fishing might be in jeopardy. Water levels in Lake Michigan and Lake Superior are gradually dropping. Lake Superior's temperature has increased 4 degrees since 1990, and if this trend continues, cold-water fish such as most trout will really find themselves up a creek, as the saying goes.

Carbon Monoxide Poisoning

Gas up your SUV again? In the last 15 years, carbon monoxide emissions in Wisconsin have increased by over 25 percent. How is this for putting things in perspective: if Wisconsin were a country, it would rank 38th on the planet (ahead of Romania and Israel) in carbon monoxide emissions, which has been pinpointed as the primary pollutant contributing to global warming.

On a Positive Note

Thank you Gaylord Nelson (of the coincidentally named Clear Lake) for making strides in improving clean air and water. Nelson had a contagiously strong interest in conserving natural resources. A state senator in 1948 and then Wisconsin's governor from 1958 to 1962, he was eventually elected to the U.S. Senate. In 1963, he embarked on an environmental tour with President John F. Kennedy, and he persuaded many other prominent politicians to get on board his crusade. It was Nelson's idea to designate one day each year to celebrate and raise awareness about the environment. Gaylord Nelson was the father of Earth Day. Every April 22, millions of people participate in programs and activities to protect the planet.

INNOVATIVE INVENTIONS

Boy Inventor Turned Father of Our National Park System

Adventurer, writer, famed naturalist—John Muir (1838–1914), who was raised near Portage, Wisconsin, was all those things. He would go on to travel to all corners of the globe, and his love of nature inspired many notable people, including his famous acquaintances such as Ralph Waldo Emerson and President Theodore Roosevelt. He personally influenced Congress to create Yosemite National Park and was instrumental in the creation of many other park preserves, such as the Grand Canyon and the Petrified Forest. However, back in the 1850s, Muir was a curious Wisconsin boy who made some remarkable inventions using sparse materials found in the northern woods. Starting with compasses and cogwheels, he moved on to complicated time-keeping devices, a working sawmill and his trademark "early rising machine" to make him get out of bed on those sluggish mornings. He was truly an almost ironic fusion of technology and nature.

Does this Test Make Me Look Fat?

In 1890, Stephen Babcock, an agricultural chemistry professor at the University of Wisconsin-Madison, debuted his milk-testing machine, which was able to gauge the percentage of butterfat in milk. It opened the door to all kinds of milk research, such as determining vitamin content levels. Next time you reach for skim instead of two-percent, know that Professor Babock had a hand in that label.

In a state know for its farming industry, it is fitting that Beloit, then Mazomanie resident John Appleby improved the grain-binding process in Wisconsin. He formed Appleby Reaper Works and patented his Appleby knotter in 1878 and his binder a year later. By utilizing twine instead of traditional wire, he revamped the methodology for grain harvesting. The vast majority of modern binding equipment used today is based on Appleby's invention.

Restless Much?

When Edward Allis moved to Milwaukee in 1846, he dabbled in leather retail, real estate and railroad investment, as well as manufacturing millstones and mining equipment before "settling down" to his own growing business, primarily designing and installing water pumps. Allis' inventions include the glamorous-sounding sewerage centrifugal pump and the plunger steam pump, which was integrated into major cities across the country and resulted in a 60-percent energy savings. All in all, Allis had over 40 patents to his name. Not content with that, he got involved with the Greenback political party and twice ran unsuccessfully for governor, in 1877 and 1881.

What Some People Will Do for Ice Cream

Ole Evinrude and his assistant/bookkeeper/eventual wife Bessie Cary were enjoying a picnic two and a half miles from the Lake Michigan shore, when Cary got a fierce craving for ice cream. Chivalrous Evinrude rowed them to shore, bought the ice cream, and then rowed them back to their picnic. Unfortunately, the ice cream had melted by then. Cursing his slow oars, Evinrude began wishing there was a faster mechanism for propelling a boat. Years later, in 1909, he introduced the first outboard motorboat engine. It was a 1.5 horsepower, gasoline-fueled single unit. In its first four years on the market, Evinrude sold almost 10,000 motors.

Evinrude reemerged over 10 years later with a new and improved version. It was a twin-cylinder motor and weighed two-thirds less than his original product. He revolutionized the outboard motor for years to come, and his company later became Outboard Marine Corporation (OMC) in Milwaukee.

The Tractor King

With the middle name "Increase," Jerome Case was destined to be successful. In 1842, J.I. Case opened the Racine Threshing Machine Works to manufacture...well, threshing machines. The company evolved over the years, became J.I. Case and Company and eventually incorporated, but their mission to produce quality products to help farmers remained consistent. They developed the first steam-engine tractor, then the first self-propelled steam engine tractor, and by 1886, J.I. Case was the largest manufacturer of steam-engine tractors in the world. About 15 years later, Case introduced its first gasoline tractor. In 1984, Case acquired its chief competitor, International Harvester, to create Case-IH. Today, Case continues to produce some of the most state-of-the-art farming equipment in the world.

Even though Christopher Latham Sholes sometimes gets most of the credit, he along with Carlos Glidden and Samuel Soule each played a part in designing the first practical typewriter in 1867. Today, the Milwaukee Public Museum holds over 700 typewriters, the largest collection in the world.

The Superman of Geeks

In the 1960s, Chippewa Falls native Seymour Cray was credited with building the first "supercomputer," the CDC 6600. In 1976, he topped himself with the creation of the CRAY-1, then the highest-performance supercomputer in the world. When he was told that Apple Computer co-founder Steve Jobs bought a CRAY to help design the next Apple, Seymour Cray's response was, "Funny, I'm using an Apple to simulate the CRAY-3."

A Sipping Cigarette

West Allis resident Brett Roth wanted to quit smoking, but cold turkey wasn't getting the job done, and he didn't enjoy the gum or the patch or any of the other options available on the market. So, in 2004, he invented his own solution—a liquid cigarette. Cleverly called Smoke-Break, the device is a clear, cigarette-shaped tube containing a liquid with about the same amount of nicotine as in your typical Marlboro Light. The "smoker" can still enjoy bringing the item to his mouth and getting a taste, but without the unpleasant smell or health risks of actual cigarette smoke. The U.S. Food and Drug Administration (FDA) has approved Smoke-Break for clinical trials.

THE GREEN BAY PACKERS

Pack Attack

If you set foot in a store or drive down the street on game day Sunday in Wisconsin, you will find everything desolate and deserted. That's because everyone is in their living rooms or at their favorite sports bar watching the game. As soon as church bells chime, green-and-gold-clad families—many of whom were undoubtedly saying prayers for a Packers victory—stream out of churches and move on to their other religion: football.

The Royal "We"

Such is Wisconsin's kinship to the sport of football that whenever Wisconsinites use the pronoun "we," they are most likely referring to the Packers (as in "We got off to a good start," or "We have a big day tomorrow").

 DID YOU KNOW?

Even though the Packers are just as famous for their green and gold colors as they are for their loyal Cheesehead fans and generation-long season-ticket waiting list, their colors actually used to be blue and gold. At one time, it was even suggested that the team name be changed to the "Big Bay Blues." But the Packers name stuck, and they have retained their name longer than any other pro football team in history. In 1950, green uniforms were issued, and the green and gold tradition began.

Starr Quote

"If you work harder than somebody else, chances are you'll beat him, though he has more talent than you."

– Bart Starr

It All Started with the Indian Packing Company

The Green Bay Packers are still the only publicly owned NFL team, thriving in a city much smaller than most professional sports teams, and their origins are just as modest. The team was conceived by a couple of average guys, George Calhoun and Curly Lambeau, in 1919. Lambeau, then a shipping clerk for the Indian Packing Company, convinced his employer to sponsor some basic equipment for the team. In tribute to that donation, they called their team the Packers. When the Packers were franchised into the American Professional Football Association, they also received financial backing from another packing company, the Acme Packing Company.

After the NFL was established, the Packers dominated during a period known as the "Iron Man Era" (because many players did not sit out even once during a game, meaning they played both offense and defense). From 1929 to 1931, the Packers from the relatively small city of Green Bay stunned their big-city rivals by winning three straight national professional football championships.

DID YOU KNOW?

The waiting list for Packer season tickets includes over 67,500 names.

A Small Man with Big Moves

Over the next 15 years, led by the NFL's first "super end," Don Hutson, the Packers prevailed in the championship three more times (1936, 1939 and 1944). Hutson was initially underestimated because of his meager 185-pound stature. Boy, were they wrong. With his swift moves and ability to change direction on a dime, Don Hutson is credited with inventing modern receiving techniques.

Some notable achievements from the man who, 50 years after his heyday, was the namesake for the Packers newly built indoor practice facility:

☛ Hutson caught a touchdown pass on his very first play as a rookie.

☛ On October 6, 1945, he scored an unprecedented 29 points in a single quarter, catching four touchdown passes and kicking five extra points.

☛ Between 1941 and 1945, he caught passes in 50 games straight.

☛ Over the course of 117 games, he scored 105 touchdowns. In all, 20 percent of his catches led to touchdowns.

☛ He was named the NFL's Most Valuable Player in 1941 and 1942, and he was invited to the all-pro team eight times.

☛ By the time Hutson retired, he held a total of 19 NFL records.

The Dream Team

When Curly Lambeau resigned as Packers coach, he was replaced by former Bears coach Gene Ronzani. It was under Ronzani's guidance, together with talent scout Jack Vainisi, that the Packers recruited some of their best players ever: Bart Starr, Ray Nitschke, Paul Hornung, Jim Taylor, Forrest Gregg and Jim Ringo. All have since been inducted into the Professional Football Hall of Fame.

A Starring Role

On January 8, 1934, a Starr was born. Though you wouldn't have known that back when he was a 17th-round draft pick! But once Bart Starr hit the field with the rest of his dream team, it was pure magic. Well, magic helped by a lot of bone-crunching hard work and unwavering determination. With Starr leading as quarterback, the Packers won six NFL championships and the first two Super Bowls ever. In fact, after a loss to Philadelphia in 1960, the Packers never again lost a playoff game while Starr was at the helm. Starr was named the MVP for both Super Bowl I and Super Bowl II.

Lombardi Wisdom

"The score on the board doesn't mean a thing. That's for the fans. You've got to win the war with the man in front of you."

– Vince Lombardi

Double Duty

When he was hired in 1959 to serve as both general manager and head coach of the Packers, few people had heard of former New York Giants assistant coach Vince Lombardi. The Packers were in a slump, having only won a single game in the season prior to Lombardi coming on board. With his inspirational words and contagious, relentless motivation, Lombardi completely turned the team around. Under Lombardi's tutelage, the Packers never had a losing season. Instead, they captured six divisional championships, five NFL championships and two Super Bowl trophies. He has since been named ESPN's "Coach of the Century."

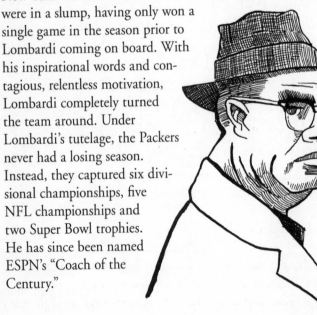

Packer Pride isn't confined to Green Bay. Inside the Radisson Paper Valley Hotel in downtown Appleton, you will find Vince Lombardi's Steakhouse, a restaurant that also serves (speaking of double duty) as a Lombardi museum. Patrons gaze at over 400 pieces of Lombardi memorabilia as they nibble the "Chocolate Super Bowl" dessert, a hollow shell of chocolate filled with strawberries and cream.

Instant Replay Game

What did officials do before technology? In a November 5, 1989, game against their longtime rivals, the Chicago Bears, Don "Magic Man" Majkowski threw Sterling Sharpe a touchdown pass with only one second left on the play clock to win the game 14–13. But line judge Jim Quirk called a penalty on Majkowski, claiming he was over the line of scrimmage when he threw the pass. It all came down to the instant replay. After several tension-filled minutes of suspense, it was declared that Majkowski's pass was legitimate, and the touchdown counted. It would be the first Packers victory over the Bears in five years.

Listen to the Coach

"Listen to what I tell you and do it. If you do, three things can happen: One, it will work and you'll get credit. Two, it won't work and I'll get the blame. Three, you'll do it wrong and you'll be gone."

– Mike Holmgren

I Am the Walrus

Because of his tusk-like mustache, many have suggested that former Packers coach Mike Holmgren bears more than a passing resemblance to a walrus. He also possesses the resourceful mammal's instinct for survival. The Packers went through many ups and downs in the latter half of the 20th century, but when

Holmgren took over in 1992, things were definitely looking up. Under his coaching, the Packers finished the season with a six-game winning streak, a feat they had not accomplished in over 25 years. The following season, Holmgren's Packers made it to the playoffs for the first time in a decade. And when they returned to the playoffs for the next five consecutive seasons, it set a new Packers record. During Holmgren's reign as coach from 1992 to 1998, the Packers won three NFC Division Championships and made two Super Bowl appearances, including their Super Bowl XXXI win over the New England Patriots. Of course, Holmgren didn't do it all on his own—some of the credit may go to his star pupil, a player by the name of Brett Favre.

DID YOU KNOW?

Brett Favre holds the record for the most NFL pass completions (5021). But his first completed NFL pass was to…himself! In Tampa Bay, in 1992, Favre's throw was deflected, and he caught the deflection for –7 yards.

All Hail to Favre

What can one say about Brett Favre that hasn't already been said? His mental and physical toughness and down-to-earth attitude have made him a hero to not just Wisconsin, but all of America. In the 2006 Harris Poll, Favre was voted the number one football player in the country (he also topped the polls in 2003 and 2004). He was even ranked third as the favorite athlete of any sport behind Tiger Woods and Michael Jordan.

Other Favre facts:

☛ Brett Favre is the only NFL player to have been named the Associated Press' MVP three times (consecutively, no less, from 1995 to 1997).

☛ Only John Elway has more quarterback wins (148) than Favre (147). And Favre is still playing. He is almost certain to exceed Elway's record during his 17th season in 2007.

☛ Favre ranks second in passing yards (57,500) and attempts (8224) behind Dan Marino.

☛ With 414 touchdown passes so far, Favre is also likely to break Marino's current NFL career record of 420 TD passes. Favre has completed more touchdown passes on the road (202) than Marino (197) or any other quarterback in NFL history.

☛ They don't get any tougher, or more dedicated, than Favre. He has started in more consecutive games (257) than any other quarterback in history. He also has the third best consecutive starts streak out of all positions in football. In 2004, *USA Today* crowned him the Number One

Toughest Athlete in Sports. That same year, *Men's Journal* magazine named him the Number One Toughest Guy in America.

☞ After a 99-yard touchdown pass to Robert Brooks in 1995, Favre attained a new (and likely unbeatable) NFL record for the longest pass completion.

☞ Favre and the Packers won Super Bowl XXXI, so Favre got his Super Bowl ring, and they brought the Lombardi Trophy (as the Super Bowl trophy has been called since 1970) back to Green Bay for the first time in 29 years. He earned his bling!

DID YOU KNOW?

Steve Young was originally cast to play Cameron Diaz's ex-boyfriend in 1998's *There's Something about Mary.* When Young bowed out, Brett Favre stepped in. Favre's cameo is indeed hilarious, though his acting has been criticized as being a little wooden. Don't quit your day job, Brett...*please*!

The Frozen Tundra

In 2007, the Packers home turf, Lambeau Field, celebrated its 50th anniversary. Some call Lambeau the "crown jewel of the National Football League," but most call it the "Frozen Tundra." And for good reason. No dome here! The stadium is completely open and exposed to the elements of a chilly football season. Part of the Packers spectator experience is freezing your buns off on the hard bleachers. The renovated stadium has seating capacity for 72,928 people, and it's always full. While other teams (wimps!) fear Green Bay's cold, icy field, the Packers excel, Favre in particular. When the kickoff temperature has been $-34°F$ or lower, Favre's home record is 40 wins and only five losses, with a 90.7 pass rating.

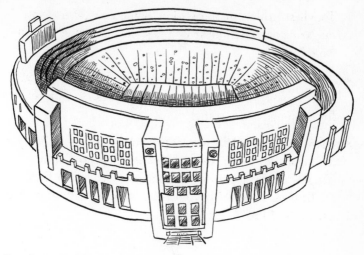

Lambeau Field's Ring of Honor includes Forrest Gregg, Mike Michalske, Willie Wood, Jim Ringo, Herb Adderley, Clarke Hinkle, Robert (Cal) Hubbard, Henry Jordan, Tony Canadeo, Don Hutson, E.L. (Curly) Lambeau, Johnny (Blood) McNally, Arnie Herber, Vince Lombardi, Willie Davis, Ray Nitschke, Bart Starr, Jim Taylor, Paul Hornung and Reggie White.

Dubbed the "Ice Bowl," temperatures at Lambeau Field dipped as low as –18°F on December 31, 1967, when the Packers faced the Dallas Cowboys in the NFL Championship game. Naturally, that didn't stop fervent fans from attending to support their team. But even with home field advantage, the game was a classic nail-biter. Nearing the end of the fourth quarter, the Cowboys were leading 17–14. A heating system that Vince Lombardi had had installed failed, and the field was an unpredictable sheet of ice. Running plays weren't working, and catching passes was just as tricky. When quarterback Bart Starr was snapped the ball on fourth and goal with just 16 seconds left on the clock, he surged forward and crossed the end zone by himself. In an unforgettable game, Starr scored the championship-winning touchdown.

DID YOU KNOW?

The first "Lambeau Leap" occurred in a game against the Los Angeles Raiders on December 26, 1993. After the Raiders fumbled the ball, it was recovered by Reggie White, who ran 10 yards before handing it off to LeRoy Butler. Butler sped 25 more yards to score the touchdown that secured the Packers a spot in the playoffs. As the fans cheered wildly, Butler ran straight toward the stands and jumped into the crowd, much to their delight. The Lambeau Leap has been a regular tradition ever since.

A TALE OF TWO TEAMS

The Braves and the Brewers

Milwaukee has been home to not one, but two major league baseball teams: the Milwaukee Braves (1953–65) and the Milwaukee Brewers (1970–present).

The Strong and the Brave

☛ Relocated from Boston, the Milwaukee Braves played their first season (1953) at the new Milwaukee County Stadium in front of a total of 1,826,297 fans—a record crowd for the National League at the time.

☛ At the end of their first season, the Braves finished in second place in the National League with an impressive 92–62 record. Hall of Famer Eddie Matthews hit 47 home runs to lead the league.

☛ The following year, then-unknown Hank Aaron (he had previously played on a minor league team in Eau Claire) debuted when the regular infielder was injured during spring training. He went on to hit 13 home runs that season.

☛ After coming in second for three of the previous four years, the Braves finally won the National League pennant in 1957 and went on to beat the New York Yankees in the World Series. With the highest number of home runs and RBIs, Hank Aaron was named MVP. That same year, Braves pitcher Warren Spahn won the National League Cy Young Award.

☛ In 1963, still standing on the mound at the overripe age of 42, Spahn set a record that he still holds today for the most wins by a left-handed pitcher. By the end of his career, he had racked up a still unrivaled 363 wins. (The next closest left-hander is Steve Carlton, who retired in 1988 with 329 wins.)

☛ In 1965, the Braves relocated to Atlanta, where they continue to play today.

DID YOU KNOW?

In 1955, only its third year with a professional baseball team, Milwaukee hosted one of the most exciting All-Star games of all time. After 12 innings, the National League managed to win 6–5. In 2002, another memorable All-Star game was played in Milwaukee at Miller Park. After 11 innings, the teams had run out of pitchers, so commissioner Bud Selig made the wildly unpopular decision to officially call the game a 7–7 tie.

The Brew Crew
☛ After a five-year hiatus without a professional baseball team in Milwaukee, the Brewers played their first game on April 7, 1970, at County Stadium in front of 37,237 fans.

☛ After a Brewers home run is scored, mascot Bernie Brewer slides down his slide and into a mug of beer. To protest lackluster ticket sales in 1970, Bernie (a.k.a. fan Milt Mason) refused to come out of his trailer until at least 40,000 fans were in attendance. Four months after their first game, attendance was sufficient for Bernie to return. The Bernie Brewer character became the official team mascot in 1973.

☛ After a bumpy beginning, both from mixed results over the previous two years and a delay in the start of the 1972 season because of a snowstorm, the Brewers wound up in first place after a 10-game winning streak, and Brewer-mania took hold.

Home Run Hero

In 1975, Hank Aaron returned to Milwaukee to play for two seasons with the Brewers (on top of the 14 years he spent with the Braves). On July 20, 1976, he hit his final home run, elevating his career home run total to 755—a record that he held until Barry Bonds broke it in 2007. (Many Aaron fans and baseball purists believe that Bonds' home runs should not count because of the widely accepted allegations of steroid use. It has been proposed that an asterisk be added next to Bonds' name in the record books).

Home Run Club

In 1975, George "Boomer" Scott led the American League in home runs, with 36 round-trippers. In 1979, Stormin' Gorman Thomas led the league with 45 home runs. He did it again in 1982 with 39 homers in total. Ben Oglivie had the most in home runs in 1980, hitting 41 balls out of the park.

One for the Record Books!

The Brewers boast three players with over 100 RBIs in two consecutive seasons: Gorman Thomas, Sixto Lezcano and Cecil Cooper in 1979, followed by Thomas, Cooper and Ben Oglivie in 1980.

Hold Onto Your Handlebar Mustache!

In 1981, Rollie Fingers became the first relief pitcher to ever win both the National League MVP title and the Cy Young Award in the same season.

So Close!

With players such as Rollie Fingers, Robin Yount, Paul "the Ignitor" Molitor, Pete "Vuke" Vuckovich, Jim "Gumby" Gantner, Cecil "Coop" Cooper, Ted "Simba" Simmons, Charlie Moore and Don Sutton all playing at peak levels, the Brewers made it to the World Series in 1982. In what is coined the "Suds Series," they lost in the end to the St. Louis Cardinals in seven games.

Lucky 13

In 1987, the Brewers set a record by winning 13 games in a row. That season, Paul Molitor had a memorable 39 game hitting streak.

Three's the Charm

Known as the "Triumphant Trio," Yount, Molitor and Gantner combined collected a Major League Baseball record 6399 hits during their careers together on the Brewers until 1999.

DID YOU KNOW?

The Milwaukee Brewers were originally the Seattle Pilots! That was until Allan H. "Bud" Selig and Edmund Fitzgerald acquired the franchise, moved them to Milwaukee and renamed them in honor of the city's beer companies and workers.

Rockin' Robin

Robin Yount began playing for the Brewers in 1973 at the tender age of 18. On August 16, 1980, he collected his 1000th hit. Over the course of the decade, Yount had more hits (1731) than any other player. In 1981, Yount was declared "Player of the

Year" by *The Sporting News.* His best year proved to be 1982, the year of Brewers made it to the World Series. Yount accomplished a career high 29 homeruns, 114 RBIs and had a batting average of .331. He also became the only player to have four hits in each of two World Series games. Rightfully so, Yount won the Gold Glove Award and was given the named the 1982 MVP. Yount's next MVP title was as an outfielder in 1989, making him the first American League player since the 1960s to earn two MVPs. In 1992, he joined an elite group of baseball players to collect over 3000 hits—an accomplishment that other baseball superstars such as Babe Ruth and Joe DiMaggio never achieved. Yount is currently ranked number 17 in all-time career hits. He was inducted into the Baseball Hall of Fame in 1999, his first year of eligibility.

DID YOU KNOW?

Yount's close teammate, Paul Molitor, is ranked ninth for all-time most career hits, with 3319. In 2004, he was finally inducted into the Baseball Hall of Fame.

Goodbye County Stadium and Thanks for the Memories
County Stadium was completely torn down and rebuilt. It reopened as Miller Park in 2001. President George W. Bush was there to toss the opening pitch.

BUCKS TOWN

The Milwaukee Robins?

When Milwaukee was approved for an NBA franchise team, a contest was held to determine a name. The most popular choice was the Robins; the Bucks name was the runner-up. The team's owners made an executive decision to go with the latter, and the Milwaukee Bucks were born.

Kareem-ing the other Teams

The new Milwaukee Bucks got off to a shaky start in 1968, finishing dead last in their first NBA season, but things soon picked up when they drafted Kareem Abdul-Jabbar. His first year, Abdul-Jabbar was named 1969 Rookie of the Year and a member of the All-Star team, the NBA All-Rookie team, Second Team Defensive and Second All-NBA team. In 1971, led by Abdul-Jabbar, the Bucks won their first and only NBA Championship. After six phenomenal years with the Bucks, Abdul-Jabbar was traded to the LA Lakers, but he still holds the record (38,387) for most career points scored—14,211 points with the Bucks, their all-time high. When Abdul-Jabbar retired, not only had he scored the most points, but he blocked the most shots, and no player at that time had ever had more NBA MVP titles (six) or been invited to more All-Star games (19).

DID YOU KNOW?

Bucks point guard Oscar Robertson is the only player in NBA history to average a triple-double over the course of an entire season. This means he scored double-digits in points, rebounds and assists. He averaged 30.8 points, 12.5 rebounds and 11.4 assists per game during the 1961–62 season. Many players never accomplish a triple-double in a single game, much less every game of a season.

NOT JUST FOOTBALL, BASEBALL AND BASKETBALL

Yes, There Are Other Sports

Milwaukee also has a professional hockey team (the Admirals) and a soccer team (the Wave). Wisconsin has also produced some other fierce athletes.

Blades of Glory

Raised in Milwaukee, speed skater Bonnie Blair won multiple medals in the 1988, 1992 and 1994 Olympic Games, making her the most decorated Winter Olympian of all time. Also at the 1994 games, speed skater Dan Jansen of West Allis won the gold medal in the 1000-meter race and set a new record.

Hailing from Madison, siblings Beth and Eric Heiden have made their mark in the sports world, particularly when the two of them combined to win half the Olympic medals awarded to the U.S. at the 1980 games. Triple-threat Beth Heiden has won four World Speed Skating Championships, the World Road Race (bicycling) and the first women's NCAA Cross-Country Skiing Championship. She also found time to earn a master's degree in civil engineering. Her speed skating big bro Eric was the first American to win the men's World Speed Skating Championship and is the only athlete to win five individual gold medals in one Olympics. He has since gone on to become an orthopedic surgeon. Talk about a family of serious overachievers!

A Wisconsin Strangler Who Wasn't a Serial Killer

Ed Lewis may be the greatest athlete you've never heard of. Born in Nekoosa, Ed "the Strangler" Lewis is considered by many to have been the best wrestler of all time—long before Hulk Hogan and friends turned the sport into more of a circus. During the 1930 and '40s, Lewis was a four-time World Heavyweight Champion. He was nicknamed the "Strangler" for his trademark headlock move. Lewis later became the first-ever Professional Wrestling commissioner. In 1951, he was inducted into the Wisconsin Athletic Hall of Fame.

"The Winningest Stock Driver in America"

Forgiving the grammar of the nickname, the title belongs to Wisconsin's own Dick Trickle, who has won over 1200 races in a career spanning 40 years. Born in Wisconsin Rapids in 1941, Trickle was born to drive. He started on dirt tracks and raced short tracks across the U.S., winning 67 races in a single season. His first NASCAR Busch Series entry was in 1984 at the Milwaukee Mile. He placed third, then elected to put his pedal to the metal on other racing circuits. After nine ARTGO championships and two ASA championships, Trickle returned to the NASCAR Busch Series and became the winningest racing legend of all time.

DID YOU  KNOW?

The Milwaukee Mile is the oldest major racetrack in the world.

The Model Driver

The 2005 Indianapolis 500 Rookie of the Year was not only a native of Beloit, but, more remarkably, was a *girl*! Since zooming to fame on the racetrack, Danica Sue Patrick has graced numerous magazine covers, including *Sport Illustrated* (the first Indy 500 *Sports Illustrated* cover ever) and sexy men's magazine *FHM* (the same magazine that ranked her the 42nd Sexiest Woman in 2005 and the 85th Sexiest in 2006), though she declined an invitation to have her picture taken for *Playboy*. In *Victoria's Secret*'s "What is Sexy" list, Patrick was named Sexiest Athlete. She has also racked up some nifty endorsements, appearing in commercials for Secret deodorant, the Honda Civic Coupe and a Go Daddy spot that aired during the 2007 Super Bowl.

DID YOU  KNOW?

The 1996 Greater Milwaukee Open at the Brown Deer Golf Course marked the professional tournament debut of golf phenomenon Tiger Woods. He tied for 60th place.

ODDS AND ENDS

The Polar Bear Club

Pretty much anyone is welcome to be a Polar Bear. The club is a popular annual tradition of bravery, stupidity or insanity, depending on your point of view. Every New Year's Day at noon, hundreds of Milwaukeeans (clothed, or at least wearing bikinis or swim trunks) charge into often-subzero Lake Michigan. Polar Bear Club president Garth Gaskey has been taking the cold plunge every year since 1952, when he and a friend came up with the concept. That's one way to cure a New Year's hangover!

Fried Bacon

No one enjoyed sunbathing more than Dick Bacon. Year-round in Milwaukee, he sported a leathery, burnt-to-a-crisp look that became his trademark. He was able to achieve this in the frosty winters by configuring enormous foil reflectors into a tent-like formation to harness the sun's rays. Besides bearing a tan that made George Hamilton appear pale in comparison, Bacon was well known for wanting to flaunt it. The frequent nude model for the Milwaukee Institute of Art and Design campaigned passionately to make part of Milwaukee's lakefront a nude beach. He lost that mission, but he did win several titles in competitive nudity and wore the crowns (and nothing else) of Mr. Nude America (1973), Mr. Nude Apollo (1976) and Mr. Nude Galaxy (1977). In August 2000, Bacon died of a heart attack, not skin cancer, while nude in his home. The sun- and volleyball-loving local character is still warmly remembered.

Not all Wisconsinites are Gun-Toting, Brat-Eating Carnivores

The Dairyland has a decent population of vegetarians, too. And while veggie-eaters in other states may eat "burgers" made of soy, black beans or a combination of ground-up grains and corn, Wisconsin has the one and only "walnut burger." The historic Trempealeau Hotel in the small town of Trempealeau created the unique nut-based alternative and has been serving this surprisingly delicious and addictive meatless meal for years. They have recently branched out, manufacturing walnut burger patties in La Crosse, and the meatless delicacy can be purchased frozen at several Wisconsin health-food stores and grocers.

Which Wisconsin woman has been a fashion model, an astronaut and a presidential candidate? The original Mattel Barbie doll of course! (In fact, she has had over 80 careers. Busy girl!) Introduced in 1959, Barbie's full name is Barbie Millicent Roberts, and her hometown is Willows, Wisconsin, where she graduated from Willows High School.

Seized Cheese

On June 4, 2007, suspicious cheese was confiscated from a traveler's carry-on bag at Milwaukee International Airport. The Transportation Security Administration confirmed that this incident mirrored others that have occurred at several major airports in the U.S., and it is possible that these were terrorist checkpoint investigations testing what they could get away with.

Apparently, the seized cheese had been packed with coils, wire, tubing and some type of initiator. In the future, if anyone is traveling with cheese (and if you visit Wisconsin, who wouldn't want to bring a wheel back home?), it is advised that you wrap the cheese tightly in clear plastic so it can be easily checked.

Off the Beaten Path

You may have heard of Hugh Hefner's famous Grotto at the Playboy Mansion. The small town of Dickeyville has its own grotto of a very different nature. Intending it to be the "biggest pilgrimage destination in the country," Father Mathias Wernerus toiled away to construct the Holy Ghost Grotto right up until his death in 1931. Combining themes of religion and American patriotism, some of the Grotto's unique features include an artificial cave, fountains, a folk art display and its trademark "Patriotism Shrine," which pays tribute to Christopher Columbus, Abraham Lincoln and George Washington. In 1963, the Stations of the Cross were added. Whether it is the biggest pilgrimage destination in the country is doubtful, but plenty of art and architecture enthusiasts and religious tourists in Wisconsin have made the trip.

Praise for Madison

☛ Best City for Cycling (population 200,000–500,000), *Bicycling,* March 2006.

☛ Best *Outside* Towns 2006: Rated Best Road Biking Town in American, *Outside,* August 2006.

☛ Third Best City in America for Walking, *Prevention,* April 2006.

☛ Fourth Brainiest Medium-Sized City, bizjournals.com, June 2006.

☛ Healthiest City in America, *Men's Journal,* 2004.

TOP TEN REASONS TO LIVE IN WISCONSIN

10. Tailgating

In other states, "tailgating" is generally a negative term that means you're riding the bumper of the car in front of you, and you could get pulled over and ticketed. In Wisconsin, tailgating is the ultimate pre-party. Hours before the game, the parking lots at Miller Park and Lambeau Field are full as people set up "camp" to tailgate. Necessities include a grill with your favorite brats or burgers, folding chairs, some music and, of course, a big cooler of beer. It's not uncommon for the Milwaukee Brewers to be dominating the third inning with the stands still sparsely populated because people are having so much fun tailgating that they don't make it to the game on time!

9. Midwestern Values

People in Wisconsin still believe in being polite. Help your neighbor. Be honest. The importance of family. People are warm and friendly and funny. Wisconsinites put a lot of stock in that.

8. Midwest Location

If you like to travel, where better to make your home base than Wisconsin? First and foremost, because it contains the hub of Midwest Express, the best airline in the world—they have made an art form of making flying coach feel like first class (must be the warm chocolate-chip cookies). You are a reasonably short, nonstop flight from both the east and west coasts. You can drive to Chicago anytime—the Windy City is the epitome of a great place to visit, but I wouldn't want to live there. You can even drive to Canada. And it might not be the ocean, but the Midwest is known for its beautiful lakes—there's something to be said for Wisconsin having two Great Lakes to enjoy.

8. The Food (yes, including CHEESE)

Cheese and cheese curds are simply delicious, and the best ones are found here in Wisconsin. Beyond cheese, we have some other delicious and unique foods derived from a variety of ethnicities and cultures: Usinger's sausage, sweet Racine Kringle, State Fair cream puffs, northern Wisconsin homemade fudge, authentic sauerkraut, and did I mention cheese already?

7. The Beer

Need I say more? And it's not exclusively your typical Miller High Life or Miller Lite (not that there is anything wrong with those!), but Wisconsin has come a long way in the variety of beer brewed here. With tasty microbreweries and up-and-comers such as New Glarus, Sprecher and Lakefront Brewery, there are plenty of cold options for washing down all that scrumptious food.

6. The Seasons

Some ironic pessimists say you need a nasty winter to really appreciate a lovely summer. Around here, people appreciate what each individual and different season has to offer. I'm not saying I enjoy shoveling, but with no snow, there would be no snowmobiling, no downhill skiing, no children making snowmen and no opening gifts in front of a cozy fire on a white Christmas morning. The transition to spring brings flowers, and people who were hibernating come out of the woodwork and are suddenly bicycling down the street or popping into shops. Kids are giddy for the school year to end. Summer in Wisconsin means lots of outdoor festivals, weekends "up north," camping, hiking and water parks at Wisconsin Dells. Along with autumn leaves and my personal favorite weather of the year, the fall offers hunting season, Packer-mania, pumpkin farms and hayrides.

5. The Dane County Farmers' Market

On Wednesdays and Saturdays, the grounds surrounding the State Capitol building in Madison are bustling with produce consumers and about 300 vendors. The air is full of energy and the smell of baked goods and fresh-cut flowers. You can purchase ripe vegetables, juicy fruit and even arts and crafts. Best of all, every agriculture-related item for sale has been produced right here in Wisconsin. The Dane County Farmers' Market is the nation's largest producer-only farmers' market.

4. The Fishing

Wisconsin's abundant lakes and countless rivers and streams are prime for fishing. If you're looking to reel in a truly impressive walleye or musky, you're more likely to catch one in Wisconsin... though that doesn't guarantee you'll get one. What fun would it be if it were easy?

3. La Fuente Mexican Restaurant

Though what I like about this place is also implied in the next item on the list, I have to single out La Fuente and give them a special shout-out. La Fuente alone is worth living in Wisconsin for. Located in the largely Hispanic-populated area of Milwaukee, the patronage of the popular restaurant is a demonstration of the improving diversity in a once strictly segregated city—it's sort of a utopian melting pot. Sitting on the restaurant's outdoor patio on any given summer night, you are surrounded by the entire spectrum of the human race: every color, religion, age and socioeconomic background are enjoying the same reasonably priced food. Maybe part of the reason everyone is so happy at La Fuente is because the margaritas are so strong—if they put that stuff in international waters there would be no war. (No, La Fuente has in no way paid me to endorse them. But if they happen to be reading this and want to offer me a margarita on the house next time I'm there, I wouldn't turn them down.)

2. Milwaukee

I admit to being biased, having lived in Milwaukee County for the better part of the last 12 years. From the fashionable and eclectic east side while attending UWM, to the inexpensive south side, back to the east side, and finally settled into a north shore Milwaukee suburb where I plan to raise my family, I've loved every apartment, flat, house and neighborhood. Milwaukee offers big-city amenities such as a great downtown with first-class performing arts and restaurants, combined with small-city accessibility. Everything I could want to do is within a 20-minute drive! I dare anyone to spend a gorgeous Saturday afternoon cruising up Lake Drive from downtown to the east side and not want to move here.

And the number one reason to live in Wisconsin is…

1. Because We Are Number One!

Wisconsin is ranked first on all kinds of other top 10 lists. We were voted as having the number one health care in the country. Middleton was named the Number One Best Place to Live in America. Even UW-Madison is number one when it comes to schools that party the hardest! The list goes on and on. I think only David Letterman has maybe seen more top 10 lists than Wisconsin has been mentioned on. Maybe.

ABOUT THE ILLUSTRATOR

Roger Garcia

Roger Garcia immigrated to Canada from El Salvador at age of seven. Because of the language barrier, he had to find a way to communicate with other kids. That's when he discovered the art of tracing. It wasn't long before he mastered this highly skilled technique, and by age 14, he was drawing weekly cartoons for a local newspaper. He taught himself to paint and sculpt, and then in high school and college, Roger skipped class to hide in the art room all day in order to further explore his talent. Currently, Roger's work can be seen in a local weekly newspaper and in places around his hometown.

ABOUT THE AUTHORS

Rachel Conard

Born and raised in Racine, Rachel Conard has been writing all her life. Her first grade teacher would let the other students "check out" her stories as if they were part of the library. And when she accompanied her father on fishing trips up north, she was more concerned about keeping her notebook dry than reeling in the 10-pound musky her dad had caught. A graduate in journalism from the University of Wisconsin-Milwaukee, Rachel loves spending time with family and friends, eating good food, enjoying a smart cocktail and playing a few party games. Her previous work has been published in Milwaukee's *Shepherd's Express*, but her main goal in life has always been to publish a book. This is her first!

Andrew Fleming

The adventurous type, Andrew Fleming is a scuba diver, ski patroller, and whitewater rafting and kayaking guide. He is also a contributing editor for *Adbusters* magazine and a freelance writer for the *Globe and Mail, Vice, Nerve, Paddler* and many other publications. Since getting his BA in English literature from McGill University, he has also studied film at Vancouver Film School and worked as an actor.